Trips on Glue

FC United of Manchester in the NPL Div 1 North 2007/8

by Steven Wood

First published in Great Britain

Published by Trips on Glue

ISBN: 978-0-9559522-0-3

Printed and Bound by Bookprinting.org.uk

In Memory of
Roy Wood and Fred Garner.
Both greatly missed by all that knew them.

Acknowledgements.

The book wouldn't have been possible without the help and support of the people below. My heartfelt thanks and appreciation goes to all of them.

To Jane, who put up with my different ideas and moments of random thoughts over and over again, Lynette Cawthra for the time and effort put in proofreading every line. John England for stats of each game, a total godsend. Nick Speakman for his superb work making my photos into such fantastic front and back covers, also to Paul Godding for setting up the website and all the hassle that went with it. I would also like to thank all at UTB for their assistance, Pete Crowther for the endless advice, Mike Duff for the fantastic poem, Alison Watt for the Riesa passage, Tony Howard for the piece in the match day programme and Robert Brady for answering various random questions by text. And to everyone who go out to play at 3 o'clock on a Saturday.

Prologue

I have never kept a diary. I have read a few (Anne Frank, Adrian Mole, Michael Palin, that bloke who got sacked as Mirror editor) but I have never actually sat down and written down my thoughts. Never seen the point really. I'll never be famous enough for people to actually be interested so there was no point. I suppose I never had the motivation neither, probably for the same reason. Well not until now.

I decided that despite not having any wish to be famous I did have some motivation. The motivation of helping my football team achieve their goal of a home of their own.

So here it is, "Trips on Glue", my diary of the 2007-08 season in the NPL Div 1 North.

It starts in preseason and takes you match by match through the season. A season where there were many incidents both on and off the pitch. I have tried my best to convey everything about what goes into a season following FC United, not just the matches, but a few of the various events that I have attended over the season.

When you are reading it, please remember it is the season seen through my eyes, so there maybe a few errors. Having said that, being a bit of a stats geek, I would be mortified if there was!! If there are, please don't stop me at a game and tell me unless you want to see a grown man cry.

I hope you enjoy reading the book. The beauty of it is you can read it however you wish. You can go from start to finish, end of season to start or just dip in match by match. S'up to you really innit, you bought it.

Oh and like all the best films, keep on right till the end, there is a nice surprise…….

Thank you loads for buying it, hope you enjoy.

Pre-season and August

The summer months are usually a quiet time for football fans. Some take the time out to go away and catch some sun, others take in the sound of willow on leather, whilst most just take the time to detox from the previous season, relax and look forward to the season ahead. That would be in a normal summer but with FC United, there is no such thing as a normal summer.

Ever since promotion and the NWCL Div 1 were secured, thoughts had turned to life in the Northern Premier League Division 1, otherwise known as the Unibond League Division 1. The main issue was how the league would be structured. The NPL wanted a league of 2 divisions, based on North and South regions but a couple of the Midland teams refused to move up into the South division. The FA backed the clubs in this, leaving a stand off between the clubs, leagues and FA. The NPL were adamant that they were going to have their 2 regional leagues. After much debate and counter debate a compromise was cobbled and put together whereby there would be 2 divisions of 18 clubs, with a commitment given to the league by the FA that by 2009, the NPL would go to a 2 league system based on regions with 21 clubs in each, as the league wished.

There were, as could be expected, problems with this system. How would the leagues be split? Would it be North/South or East/West? As there would only be 18 teams in each league, it would mean only 34 games over the season. Would the games be made up in some way? Could the clubs afford to play just the 34 games in the season? Maybe the league would just introduce another cup competition to make up the shortfall?

What actually happened, seemed to verge on the farcical.

The league was split on a North/South basis. When the split actually occurred, teams such as Cammell Laird, Colwyn Bay and Sheffield, who would consider themselves in the north, were put in the southern division. This of course upset these teams due to the extra travelling they would need to do, as well as missing out on the money they may have expected when the FC circus rolled into town. To be fair, it did seem weird that FC and Woodley were in the northern division, but Warrington went into south. I suppose there must be some logic to it, but it isn't easy to see to the untrained eye.

The next dilemma facing the league was the number of games to be played. As they hadn't got their preferred number of teams, it had to be decided how many games were to be played, and if the decision was 42 games where would the extra 8 games come from? The decision that came was strange to say the least. During the season, teams would play everyone home and away once as would be expected, but then the league would be split into two. The split would be done on a regional basis, so teams wouldn't be travelling too far for these games and would be played on a basis that 4 games would be at home, 4 games away making up the 8 game shortfall. These "mini leagues" wouldn't actually be leagues in themselves, the results would go towards the main NPL Div 1 North. So in effect the championship could actually be decided on a postcode lottery and not necessarily on the pitch. Take for example two teams at the top of the league, one team plays their extra games against teams near the top of the table, one plays the games against teams at the bottom. It would seem on the face of it, one team has an advantage over the other based on where they are located and not how good they are on the pitch. Of course this is a simplistic way of looking at it, and football doesn't usually follow logic like that.

Hopefully the league won't live to regret the decision to make up the extra 8 games, having 34 games would have given plenty of time to allow for postponed games, as well as any cup runs that clubs may go on.

It was only known when the fixtures came out who FC would be playing in the extra games. It turned out to be that the extra home games would be against Woodley Sports, Rossendale United, Chorley and Lancaster City. The extra away games would be at Bamber Bridge, Radcliffe Borough, Clitheroe and joy of joys, Skelmersdale. It seemed to be wait and see time with regard to the crowds these clubs get on the second FC visit. Would the FC fans follow the team on the second time they played those grounds? Will the reserves see an upturn in their attendances that day? Only time would tell.

Amongst all this there was another historic day in the life of FC United, as for the first time we were entered into the draw for the FA Cup. The draw was on paper kind to FC, as it paired the club with either Trafford or Atherton LR, both teams from NWCL Div 1. A trip to the seaside would be on the cards for the winners, as the draw then paired them with Fleetwood in the 1st qualifying round.

At the same time, the FA Trophy draw was made, and another away tie, this time at Bradford PA. Should we get the win there, we will face the oldest club in the world in Sheffield FC.

The League Cup draw gave us a home tie with Alsager in the 1st round of the challenge cup and the President's Cup paired FC with Bamber Bridge at home.

So with the league sorted and the draws for the myriad of cups made, it was finally time for the football to begin, starting with Studley FC away.

Bring on United!!

14th July 2007
Studley FC 1 FC United 2 (Patterson 4, 20)
Attendance: Approx 500

The game at Studley was arranged in aid of the Jimmy Davis memorial fund. Jimmy was of course the Manchester United player who died in a car crash in August 2003 whilst on loan at Watford. Every year, a game takes place in memory of Jimmy and to raise funds for charity. In the past clubs such as Swindon, Watford and WBA have all played in aid of the fund, and in 2007, FC United was asked to take part.

The day started early, as we planned to leave in good time to miss any traffic and get down for a few early shandies pre game. So off we went onto the M6 with no problems at all. As we approached Birmingham the question was to toll or not to toll? In true FC fashion, it was decided that "nah, balls to it, be reet, £3 is price of a beer" so we continued on our merry way, till we reached Hilton Park services that is. Thirty minutes and 3 miles later, we were still sat in the traffic, starting to curse and clock

watch, with valuable pre match drinking time being lost. It lightened our mood of course, when we finally got through it, only to see that the hold up was actually just a minor 3 car bump, and not road works. Finally after around 2 and half hours, we finally arrived at Studley's ground.
Entrance to the game was £5, and a programme £1. Usually I don't bother with away programmes, especially friendlies, but with it being such a worthy cause, it was an essential purchase.
After the game, there was an auction of signed football memorabilia, donated by the likes of MUFC, WBA, Chelsea, Birmingham City and of course FC United. It is good to see that even in this day and age, football clubs can come up trumps with donating stuff to raise funds elsewhere. There was a signed Ole Gunnar and Ryan Giggs shirt, as well as 2 signed balls. The plum lot, I suppose, would be the signed David Beckham LA Galaxy shirt, this wasn't on show sadly, but I presume that it would be sent on. A nice touch by Mr Beckham I thought, to remember Jimmy and donate something as valuable as that to the auction.
After a few beers and catch up with faces not seen since the end of last season, it was finally time for the new season to kick off.
The teams were lead out by FC's very own Alex and Lucy Croft, always a nice touch to have them lead out the teams. FC lined up in their white and black away shirts, so no sign of the new home shirt as yet, despite Studley wearing blue. The team contained just one new face, Dale Whitehead, previously of Salford City lining up in midfield, and with Matty Taylor, Alex Mortimer and Chaddy all missing from the back line, the ever dependable Spenner played at right back, Adam Turner partnered Nugent in the middle with Sean Roscoe at left back. Anthony Hargreaves the other new face in the squad, started on the bench.
It didn't take long for FC to take control of the game, and for Rory Patterson to get off the mark in spectacular fashion, curling the ball in the net on the half volley from the corner of the box. The general opinion round us being if he carries on like this, he will be this pre-season's Torpey and be off to a higher

level. The score was doubled again by the man Patterson, this time coolly slotting the ball past the debutant Studley keeper.
It seemed like the game was over, FC looked comfortable on a hard bumpy pitch, which considering the monsoon it had had on it during the "summer" was some doing. The only question would be how many changes would Margy make at half time?
As expected there were changes on both sides, with Margy only keeping on Josh, Nuge, Roscoe and Turner from the first half. This made for, to be honest, a pretty dull half, with only really Lee Ellis enjoying himself, by seemingly trying to break the record for most sitters missed in one game. Maybe a little harsh, especially from the sidelines, but it seemed like he was hell bent on putting the ball wide and over, as opposed to actually in the net.
Clearly the management started to get bored, so Margy decided to liven it up by bringing Rory back on at left back. I reckon, in the future and when his legs start to go a little, he can find himself an Indian summer playing at left back, nothing looked like getting past him, he was calm on the ball, and his crossing superb.
Studley pulled one back, as the ref decided to try to even it up by awarding a dubious (well it looked like dodgy from the other end) penalty, but FC held on for a victory and the 1st silverware of the season.
The presentation took place on the pitch, as medals were handed out to both teams, the silver cup presented to Josh Howard who was captain in the second half, and the M-O-M award that was given, bizarrely in my view to Howard, hopefully he had the grace to hand it over to Rory in the dressing room. A nice touch was to present Alex and Lucy with medals as thanks for being mascots, the pride on their faces was a sight to behold.
The auction took place after all the trophies were handed out, the top bid being £1,000 for the signed Beckham shirt, well worth it given it must be one of the first ones to have been donated, and of course given the more than worthwhile cause,
A couple of days after the game, the grand total raised was announced. The clubs and supporters of both Studley FC and FC

United can be proud that £5496 was raised on the day for Acorns Hospice for terminally ill children and When You Wish upon a Star Charity.

22nd July 2007
Blackpool Mechanics FC 1 FC United 2 (Wright 21, Patterson 86)
Attendance: Approx 500

The next game due to be played was away at Kidderminster Harriers, but thanks to the bad weather, the game was called off, and put back a week, so the reserve friendly at Blackpool Mechanics took on more of a first team feel.
Some of the Prestwich lads had been up to Blackpool the previous week in order to sort out possible camping facilities, such was the success of the camping in Barrow at the end of the previous season. Confirmation came back that camping was fine at the side of the pitch, and there would be toilet and washing facilities available. It was game on, the car was packed and off to Blackpool the day before the game.
On arrival at the Mechanics ground, we found the advance party already set up, the Prestwich lads had been there since Thursday, and with a couple of others arriving on the Friday.
On the way up, we were wondering if it was such a good idea to camp as the heavens seemed to be coming in on the M61, but as Blackpool was approached, the weather was pretty clear, so with slight reservations, the camping equipment was laid out. Of course and as expected, sod's law kicked in, as the rain that we encountered on the motorway made its way over to Blackpool, so the tent was put up in the pouring rain, with the ground getting all the more muddy, and us getting wetter and wetter. And yes, as expected, as soon as the tent was up, the rain stopped.
Once everything was up, we retired to the Shovels pub over the road, with our new camping neighbours.
We ordered our drinks, and took seats in the pub, to be greeted with the words "Ahh FC United". Now as far as I could see,

none of us were at that point wearing any FC clothing, and we didn't have the words tattooed on our heads, so it seemed a little weird that someone should pick up on this. It turned out that these lads were officials and players from Squires Gate FC, who we had played last season. We sat down, and chatted to them about FC, the local non-league scene in general and also the games v Blackpool Mechanics in the first season, especially the one in Blackpool, that made a tidy sum for the home side that they used to purchase a new posh lawn mower for the pitch.

The rest of the night was spent eating from the BBQ and having a few beers sat in front of the tent and watching the impromptu game of football in the dark taking place on the pitch. Well, a game that was happening until a visit from who we presumed was an official of Blackpool Mechanics, who asked us if we felt it fair that people were playing football on the pitch that they had got ready for the game. To be honest, everyone playing was wearing flat trainers and only actually playing in one goalmouth, so personally I didn't see a problem with it, but everyone was called off the pitch, and that was pretty much the end of the evening festivities. I can't help but think that the Mechs had missed a trick, not asking one of their bar staff to open up the clubhouse for us, it would have kept people off the pitch and put money over the bar that they wouldn't have had usually, but their club, their rules I suppose.

After a rainy night, with every drop of rain hitting the tent and it sounding like a monsoon, it was time to get sorted for the game. Everyone on the site had pretty much said that they were packing up and going straight home after the game, so we decided that we would do the same, and as with the previous afternoon, the tent was put away in the rain, which didn't help the mood too much.

The club hadn't officially arranged any transport to the game, with it being a Sunday and originally a reserve friendly, and the boogie bus and meet up in the Old Bridge, scene of events after the previous Mechanics game, also cancelled. We made our way into Blackpool, and shortly after parking up the car, a miracle occurred. No, not all the stag and hen parties that litter the

streets of Blackpool being vaporised, and the chain theme pubs turning into real ale houses, the sun came out. Yes, the bright yellow sky thing finally made an appearance.
Trade at the Old Bridge was brisk, it certainly wasn't as full as it would have been if the game had been on a Saturday, but some decent money will have gone over the bar pre-game.
As we were leaving the pub, to get some scran in the chippy next door, there was a fly past by the Red Arrows, with the clear blue Blackpool sky making the perfect backdrop.
As kick off time approached, it was time to drive back to the ground and have the usual pre match drinks in the clubhouse. It was here that we heard Stuart Rudd had broken his hand the day previous and would be out for around 6 weeks. There was also a last minute team change, as Josh Howard had to pull out due to an allergic reaction to the sand that had been put on the pitch to help it to dry out. This made his goal in the cup final all the better, considering that that Curzon pitch that night was probably around 70% sand.
The team was a mix of first team and reserve players with new signing Anthony Hargreaves making his maiden start in a FC shirt and Jerome Wright making his first pre-season start.
To be honest, the game never really got going too much. There wasn't much goal mouth action at all, until the end of the half, when a superb cross from Dave Swarbrick was volleyed in at the far post by Wright, though his celebration seemed to suggest that it came off his shin.
Margy made a few changes at half time, taking off the impressive Nicky Platt and also Sam Ashton, allowing John Ogden a chance in goal. Unfortunately, he didn't have too great a start, as an attempted clearance up field rebounded off a Mechs player and into the empty net to make the score 1-1. This set back didn't deter the singers in the bus stop behind the goal, and they continued to sing non stop, fuelled no doubt by the bracing sea air, or possibly the hospitality in the Old Bridge.
The game continued in a similar vein as the 1st half, with FC having most of the play, but not really finding much of a way through the Blackpool defence.

Margy also seemed to be a little frustrated by this, so he sent on his super sub, Phil Power in order to up the effort and entertainment. As usual, he didn't disappoint. Within just a few minutes of coming on, he was pulled up by the referee for a foul, that clearly he didn't agree with. You could see it in his eyes, the Power was unhappy, he glared at the ref, the play restarted, one of the Mechs players stopped on the touchline with the ball at his feet, the Power close behind. This seemed to be a mistake, especially as out of the corner of my eye, I could see Phil coming, still with that look in his eye. Still the Mechs player stood, looking for the killer ball into the box. Sadly for him, he never actually managed to make it, as Power charged straight into the back of him, with a very loud thud. The player collapsed to the ground, the ref came over, and went straight for the yellow card. The mist seemed to lift from the Power's eyes, his revenge had been served. He was happy.
The game was won in the last couple of minutes by the ever lively Rory Patterson, who bobbled a low shot past the keeper to seal a 2-1 FC victory.

29th July 2007
Kidderminster Harriers FC 1 FC United 1 (Patterson 41)
Attendance: Approx 676

The biggest pre-season test for FC came away to Kidderminster Harriers of the Conference. This game would give a good indication of how FC would do in the coming season. Would they be able to step up another level and compete? The performance at Kiddy would give a good indicator of that. As with the higher level of opposition, came a higher level of admission price, £10 being charged for a pre-season game.
On my travels so far, I have made many a comment on and indeed eaten many a pie, hot dog and burger from the various outposts we have visited, but never have I seen anything similar to what was on offer at the Aggborough Stadium. For the price of four of your English pounds, a cottage pie could be purchased. Yes, a whole bone fide cottage pie. With mince, veg,

and golden brown mashed potato on top. Sadly I didn't think I could manage to eat a full one due to them looking like the side of a bus, so I had to pass by on this pie heaven, but the way they were being purchased and devoured suggested to me that Kiddie had played a blinder. Shame I couldn't say the same for the rather bland burger that I plumped for.

There were round about 250 Fc'ers in attendance, and from my vantage point in the seats, it sounded like 2500. The acoustics from the stand were superb and every song came over loud and clear. The same couldn't be said from the fans in the other end, but I suppose this game wasn't such a big deal to them, playing a team a couple of divisions down in the pyramid.

The ground itself was pretty tidy, 2 seated stands down each touchline and a covered terrace at each end. Both these had pretty low roofs, and so the sound was superb. Something to consider and remember in the future I should think.

FC started brightly and confidently, and were certainly playing the better football, but without much success. The deadlock was broken shortly before half time, as Rory went clean through and slotted the ball into the bottom corner.

The joy on the terrace didn't last long though as ex MUFC keeper Smikle equalised in front of the home fans.

The 2nd half was also pretty even, and not the most eventful of games, when I noticed a familiar face walking over to take a throw in front of us. It was none other than ex Blackburn player Jeff Kenna. Now I am not usually one for dishing out abuse to opposing players (unless of course they try to break the legs of one of our lads) but there was always something about Kenna that I just didn't like. Totally irrational, but then again they are always the best hatreds. Anyhow, it was a moment that I really didn't want to pass on, and in a rare moment of genius, this beauty was born:

Jeff Kenna, Superstar
He's won just as much
As Alan Shearer.

Sadly, and to my great dismay, it didn't catch on.

FC could have actually won the game late on, as Rhodri Giggs went through and tried to round the keeper, who did well to recover and take the ball off his feet.
The game ended 1-1, and was a good run out. The FC players did themselves and the fans proud with a good performance and certainly gave hope for a successful season in the NPL.

31st July 2007
Trafford FC 2 FC United 1 (Swarbrick 63)
Attendance: 406

Last season, one of the teams to give us most trouble was Trafford. A scruffy 1-0 win at Alty was followed by an exciting 4-4 draw at Gigg Lane towards the end of the season. With this in mind, and with the knowledge that quite a few of the Trafford players had left to join their ex-manager at Ashton United, we approached the game at Shawe View not really knowing what to expect, but confident that a win would be the outcome.
On arrival at the ground, it was straight into the tidy and compact clubhouse, and over a pint of weak Aussie lager, the usual routine when old team photos are on show of looking to see any of our lads. A couple of pics showed Chris Simms and Billy McCartney on them, there could have been more, but I was drawn more to pics of Trafford pictured before previous finals of the Manchester Premier Cup, with one of them at Old Trafford, hmmmm could be interesting.
We took our seats in the tiny stand and settled down to see Trafford take control of the game, and go into an early lead. FC just didn't seem to get into the game at all, though a couple of players were playing their first pre-season game in the first team, and a couple were out of position, so this may account for the disjointed nature of the performance.
At half time, the score was still 1-0 to the home side, with a bit of thinking to do from Margy. Five changes were made in the side, but with no clear improvement in performance, especially as Trafford capitalised on a mistake to make the score 2-0.

The game was just drifting along with Trafford playing the better of the two teams and FC huffing, puffing and getting nowhere. That was until Mr Patterson decided to take things by the scruff of the neck….quite literally.
He had earlier been flattened when bearing down on goal, and blasted a good chance into the side netting but after a late tackle on the touchline, the red mist descended. During a scuffle involving a number of players, he got involved with one of the Trafford players, raised hands from both sides, and the words "You and me now" repeated over and over again in a broad Irish accent.
The inevitable red cards followed, but in his wisdom, the ref decided to issue them together. This only resulted in both players leaving the field at the same time, and continuing their spat all the way off the pitch, and to the tunnel where Rory was finally escorted to the dressing rooms.
Incidents like this were common in the first season, when at times I thought that Rory let his team-mates down with what seemed to be a rash temper and greediness in front of goal. In the second season, this seemed to go, as the sublime skills that he showed at times in the first year, came to the fore and the snarling, unhappy looking, "everyone is against me" persona took a back seat. Only time will tell if the Trafford incident was a one off or a return to the olden days, but to be honest all the better players in the past had a streak in them, and to be honest no one wants a team of Linekers, Rory would probably be half the player if he lost that little bit of devil.
The incident seemed to galvanise FC, and Dave Swarbrick a pulled goal back, which led to an onslaught on the Trafford penalty area. The crossbar was rattled by Chaddy, and with better finishing, in truth much better finishing, Swarbrick would have finished with a hat-trick.
As it was, the game finished in a 2-1 loss, which gave plenty of food for thought for Margy and the fans, especially with a potential rematch looming in the FA Cup early in the season.

4th August 2007
AFC Wimbledon 2 FC United 0
Attendance: 2112

It is a matter of record that AFC Wimbledon were a huge help in the early days of FC United, it could even be argued that if it wasn't for their help, advice and guidance, we wouldn't have a club to call our own. The friendship between club officials and supporters is warm, and this is reflected in a seemingly annual friendly game. The first to take place down at Kingsmeadow (as it was named in those days) was won by AFC with a single goal. The return at Gigg was won 2-1 by FC thanks to a great goal by the soon to depart Steve Torpey. The question was who would go ahead in the series of games?
The day started very early, 5.15 am early, as we had to be up to get the coach down to that London. The club had managed to find us a couple of seats on it at the last minute, but this was in exchange for stewarding the coach on the way down. It was the first time I had done this, and to be honest having seen Blackie do it on the monkey bus, and Mark and Peanut have a go on the few occasions I have travelled on the FC coach, it seemed a bit of a hassle and faff, but I agreed.
The first job of a steward is to check that everyone on the list is on the coach. Of course, this brought the first problem of the day, as 2 places were unaccounted for. After an attempt to ring, which resulted in a dead line, a shout to the bus to see if anyone knew the said person, brought the shout from the back, "She isn't coming!!" It's nice when people let you know I suppose.
The second task is to collect the money from the passengers. This was surprisingly painless, apart from one fan who tried to rip off his own club by paying a kid's price instead of an adult. He may have got away with it as well if it wasn't for the fact that he is pissed at every game we play and that I was stood next to him at Studley when he was telling all and sundry that he had celebrated his 21st birthday the day before. Still as I said to him, ten out of ten for trying.

One eventless journey and Bond film later, we were pulling up at the "Cherry Red Records fans' Stadium" just as the clubhouse was opening its doors.

The game started off in a similar vein to the Trafford one, with AFC playing all the football, and FC on the back foot. It looked ominous for FC when the ref gave an early pen against Chaddy after a tussle in the FC box. Thankfully (and not for the last time during the game) Sam pulled off a save.

It was inevitable that the Wombles would score first, and they did thanks to a glancing header. Something then happened that I would never have expected. Music was played over the PA. Our brethren, our mentors, our strength in the dark days of 2005 were actually playing music after they scored. This was topped off with a giant Womble dancing in the main stand. At first I stood there in astonishment, and then cracked up laughing. But it was a surprise.

A mistake on the FC right led to AFC taking a 2-0 lead just before half time, and this time, thankfully no music.

Margy again rang the half time changes, and this seemed to have an effect early in the second half as first Rory, then Giggs had chances to pull a goal back. Sadly neither went in and as the half went on, it was AFC who got back on top and it was left to Sam in goal to keep them out with a number of saves that rightly earned him the Man of the Match award, following in the footsteps of Barrie George who won it at the last game at Wimbledon.

As we sat on the coach after the game, thoughts turned to the last couple of performances and results. Usually pre-season games don't mean too much apart from a chance to get the players fitness up to speed, hopefully that is what the last couple of games were all about and not too much can be read into them when the season begins.

I can't let this section go though, without a mention of a few thoughts on the day of what I had seen and heard. We all know that we have a common bond with AFC, they had their club taken from them and moved, many of us feel Glazer took our club from us, both clubs were formed under similar ideals, but

the game brought home that we don't share the same appeals and principles. Their ground has been renamed with the moniker of a sponsor, a deal the commercial manager said was the greatest deal he had done. They have shirt sponsors as well, something that many many FC'ers are totally opposed to. There is no problem with these things of course, if that is what Wimbledon wish to do, it is their club after all, but does give you a reminder of how FC is different in ideals from even its closest ally. As for the music after the goal, the Womble on the pitch and drum being banged on the terrace, sadly these are seen by myself as the worse excesses of 90s football and I for one hope they are never seen at FC in my lifetime.
It was announced on the Monday after the game, that Rhodri Giggs had been released from the club. I am sure he will be happy playing for his proper club.

11th August 2007
Ashton Utd 1 FC United 4 (Wright 3, Hargreaves 9, Patterson 20 pen 73)
Attendance: 624

The final pre season game took us to one of our regular outposts, Ashton but this time to play Ashton United of the Unibond Premier League. This was the first outing of the new FC shirt which is very similar to the 1977 FA cup final shirt worn by MUFC. It's also a nice touch to see that the numbering on the back of the FC shirt is done in a retro fashion, well done to whoever decided on that one.
With 2 mins gone in the game, FC went ahead thanks to an Ashton defensive mix up, and Jerome Wright slotting the ball home. FC was the better team, and it was no surprise when they went 2-0 up thanks to Anthony Hargreaves's 1st goal in a FC shirt, nodding in a rebound from a Patterson freekick. It was 3-0 on 20 mins as a Howard run ended in the ref pointing to the spot, Patterson doing the honours. Ashton came into the game more in the 2nd half, but a couple of decent saves from Sam kept them at bay. Rory ended the game on 73 mins as he slotted

home no 4. Ashton did pull one back towards the end, but it was to no avail. An excellent performance all round from FC, especially on the back of the Trafford and Wimbledon games.

18th August 2007
Lancaster City 2 FC United 1 (Wright 90)
Attendance: 2257

Sadly I missed this game as I was attending the V Festival. I had also missed the first ever FC home game against Padiham back in 2005 due to the very same reason. Damn these late summer music festivals. My intention of this section was that there would be lots of goals and I could note them as they happened thanks to texts and also say who was on stage at that point. But as usual best laid plans and all that, meant that all the goals were scored in stoppage time, one at the end of the first half (I was watching Mark Ronson at the time do his set of covers) and two at the end of the second half, that I had to chase the info for, thinking that my contact had forgotten. He hadn't, just not had time to let me know. At that point I was stood watching The Fratellis plod through some heavy rock dirge.

22nd August 2007
FC United 0 Garforth Town 1
Attendance: 2216

Garforth Town from Lids were the opponents for the first NPL home game. They came out in their Brazil style Yellow and Green kits, presumably in honour of when Socrates played a match for them. Sadly, this is where the similarity started and ended, as they played more like Uruguay circa Mexico 86. They had obviously come out with a game plan, if it wears red and it moves, put it to the ground. And it worked!! They had done their homework, as early on Patterson came in for some rough treatment, one "hard" challenge resulted in him limping off the field, he came back for 10 mins, but couldn't continue, and was

last seen leaving Gigg Lane with the sirens going and blue lights flashing.
As I had missed the Lancaster game, this was my first sight of the Unibond League patches on the sleeves of the shirt. There had been much discussion about these since the end of the previous season, some were totally against wearing them, whilst some said it wasn't sponsorship and so wasn't a problem. Personally, whilst I would prefer to see nothing on the shirt at all, I could see that this wasn't sponsorship of the club, which I had perceived us to have voted no on previously, and so it wasn't a major problem. Also, there would be penalties connected with not wearing them, both financially, which quite frankly the club can't afford to take, as well as regarding points and our position in the league. These challenges will come up over and over as the club progresses and grows, and as long as the members have their say on these matters, as we did with the NPL patches, then everything will be done in the correct manner, and the people who matter the most have made the decision.
Back to the game and Braz….Urugu…..erm Garforth were still doing their best "If it moves, make sure it moves no further" routine and sadly, the referee seemed unable, or unwilling to do anything about it. As an ex-referee, I am sometimes loathe to criticise refs too harshly, it is a difficult thing to do, something that you can only really appreciate if you have done it, but this gentleman just seemed to be enjoying himself just a little too much in front of the 2000+ crowd. He was letting heavy challenges go and penalising the smallest bit of contact. This is something guaranteed to annoy players and spectators alike. This was summed up perfectly when Stuart Rudd was kicked about two feet in the air and play was waved on, only for seconds later, Rob Nugent to pick up a booking for not even touching a Garforth player. The crowd were unhappy with the ref, and let him know, though I do personally wish that "You don't know what you're doing" would be left to the likes of Derby County and Southampton. Amidst all this mayhem,

Garforth took the lead with a break away from the incessant FC pressure.
FC were totally on top in the game, but couldn't get a breakthrough, the ball was flying across the box, shots being blocked desperately, and the ref was slowly but surely losing the game. This was proven when Stuart Rudd was caught as he chased a ball out of play, a melee ensured and two red cards were shown, one to the Yorkshire South American touring side, one to Rudd seemingly for the crime of being on the end of a boot in the chest.
This galvanised FC and the pressure became an onslaught. The ball was getting nearer and nearer but it just wouldn't go in. Shots were blocked and kicked off the line, headers were tipped over by the keeper, and when the ball finally did get put into the net, the flag went up for offside. It was clear that it wasn't to be FC's night. At the final whistle, the Garforth team celebrated as if they were the Brazilians winning the WC in 1970, with one or two players coming over to the MRE to beat their chests like gorillas. You can take a lad out of Leeds I suppose........
More of a worry was the attacking options for Margy, as Rudd looked set for a 3 game ban, and Patterson out injured for a few weeks. Still as we always say "In Margy we trust."

25th August 2007
FC United 6 (Patterson 16 23 64 75, Hargreaves 83, Taylor 89 pen) Bridlington Town 0
Attendance: 2253

The talk after Garforth was how refreshing it was to watch a game that was keenly fought and close. Whilst of course there had been close games in the previous adventures in the NWCL, all too often games were finishing 4-0, 5-0 and higher. With this in mind, Bridlington rode into Gigg Lane and went home with a 6-0 defeat. It was just one of those games where finally everything fell right. The ball didn't just fly backwards and forwards across the goalmouth, it finally hit its target. Star of the show was Rory Patterson, with a 4 goal haul, made all the more

amazing since he was last seen leaving Gigg in an ambulance with a suspected fractured foot.
It was a superb performance from FC, with the old style midfield partnership of Spencer and Carden dominating as they had done so often in the past. It was, though, one of the new faces, Anthony Hargreaves who stood out with his non-stop running and working for the team, which produced a superb cross for the FC 2nd goal, and him actually scoring the 5th. There was even time for a pantomime, when FC was awarded a penalty. It looked as if Rudd was going to take it at first then sensibility seemed to prevail, as the usual taker Platt stepped forward and put the ball on the spot. Sensible until the red sea parted, and from nowhere strode Matty Taylor to try his luck. After a few words, he respotted the ball, and slotted it home for his first ever FC goal. It couldn't have been anymore farcical if the Chuckle brothers had turned up to have a go at taking it, but as it was already 5-0, and was scored, I don't suppose it really matters.
Later that evening, a few FC'ers had a night at the theatre. Not a usual post match event it has to be said, but it was the final night of "She just nipped out for fags", a production put on by the Moston Active Drama group or MaD, at the Library Theatre in Manchester.
This group had been introduced to FC by Gary Selvidge who had made contact with them through local Manchester author, Mike Duff. MaD had come down to FC in the past, to do some workshops with the FC juniors and take in a match. It only seemed fair that their performance was supported by FC if possible and over its 3 night run, many FC supporters had gone along to watch.
The story was based around a family who had to cope with the mother going to the shop, and not coming back, and the family, who were all United mad, managing to hold it all together with the help of the next door neighbour, who is a drag queen.
As you can imagine, the play had some very funny moments, but one or two poignant ones as well, especially the scene after the grand-dad had died, and the dad was speaking at the funeral.

It took me back to earlier in the year, when I was doing the very same thing at my dad's own funeral.
The production was superb, with faultless performances from the actors in the show, even more remarkable considering that the bulk of them were youngsters, I predict big things for one or two of them for sure.
In the play there were two mentions of FC. One at the start, in a throwaway line about collecting for charity outside football grounds, and a major one right at the end of the play, when all is resolved and the mother comes back to the family (via a trip to America and a marriage to someone on death row.) The kids are promised a day out at United, not Man United but FC United, where the football is fun and affordable. This line got a decent cheer from certain audience members. The play ended with a montage of photos, including a good number taken on a match day down at Gigg Lane, with the MAD kids enjoying their day out.
The play was devised and written by Rob Lees and Jill Hughes, both of whom appear in the play, and the best recommendation I can give is that I intend to see all future performances by MAD and I heartily recommend them. Hopefully the relationship built between them and FC United will continue to grow in the future.

27th August 2007
Rossendale United 1 FC United 2 (Rudd 71, Platt 82 pen)
Attendance: 2023

It makes a big difference when a home team pull out all the stops to welcome FC and all its followers to its ground, and it's safe to say that Rossendale United totally excelled themselves on the August Bank Holiday. They laid on a fun day for all the family that included a lazerzone and beat the keeper, decent BBQ on which, for a change, tasty, juicy burgers were cooked, a chilled bottled beer stall, decent ales in the clubhouse and an Irish band which, whilst not really to my tastes, went down a treat with most others, especially when Kitman George gave a rendition of Bar Scarves Twirl. Everyone outside the ground seemed to be enjoying the festivities laid on and this led onto a good atmosphere during the game. Many fans had travelled on the East Lancs steam railway to the game, as they had done to Ramsbottom the previous season. People always say things aren't as good second time around, and with this in mind, we chose to drive to the game, but the feedback coming from the rattler travellers was that the trip was just as good as the previous one.

On the pitch, the game was strangely slow, especially after the blood, guts and goal fests of the previous two games. FC were on top in terms of possession, but couldn't get the breakthrough, with Rossendale happy to soak up the attacks and break. On a couple of occasions, they almost caught the FC backline out, but a couple of saves from Sam in goal made sure there was no score at half time.

After the break, the pace seemed to pick up a little, Steve Spencer had a good chance cleared off the line and Rossy had the best chance of the game, but their striker could only fire wide when left open in front of goal.

This miss seemed to fire the Reds into action, and on 71 mins, a Stuart Rudd freekick from outside the box somehow went through a mass of bodies and crossed the line. The relief was total on Rudds face, as he had finally broken his duck for the season.

Some sloppy FC defending allowed Rossy to pull it back to 1 all soon after, for some reason the lads seemed to take their collective feet off the gas. Maybe it was the fact that for some reason, the crowd behind the goal were singing more about Man ciddy than FC.

Just after 80 mins, a long ball into the box towards Ruddy saw him manhandled by a Rossy defender, and the inevitable penalty was awarded. Thankfully the shenanigans of the previous game were avoided, and Nicky Platt slotted the ball home to make it 2-1.

The game really pretty much petered out after this, as FC calmed the game down, and Rossy seemed to have the wind taken out of their sails and FC holding on for an important win.

September 2007

2nd September 2007
FA Cup: Preliminary Round
Trafford FC 2 FC United 5 (Nugent 11, Howard 17, Platt 44 pen, Carden 69, Hargreaves 90)
Attendance: 2238

September started with probably the most eagerly anticipated game since Leigh RMI in 2005, with FC finally entering the FA Cup at the final preliminary round.
In the build up to the game, the FA Cup was brought to an open training session held by the club at MANCAT, where people could watch the lads go through their paces, have photos with the cup, and in some cases become media whores and get their fizzogs on Granada Reports.
Sadly for myself, due to a very pressing family matter, I couldn't attend, so the cup fever really only got going for me on the morning of the game. There was always an extra spring in my step on FA Cup days in the past, and this was no different. It always feels different when you know you are going to watch an FA Cup game, probably due to the fact that when I started to watch the Reds that was the only trophy we were ever likely to win.
The romance of the cup (that's one cliché got in!!) made sure we were up to the ground nice and early, and with the bar in the boozer next to the ground 6 deep, we decided to get into the ground early and soak up the cup atmosphere. It looked like others had had the same idea, as there were already quite a few in the ground, reading programmes, watching the lads warm up and eating pies as early as 2 pm.
Soon, the side down the pitch began to fill up, and it became apparent that the segregation put in place wasn't really needed, so the tape was lifted and the FC choir filled the covered sections down the side of the pitch, and behind the goal.
From the kick off, FC were the better team, Trafford looking nervous especially at the back and it came as no surprise that we took the lead thanks to the ginger nut of Rob Nugent. Now, if there was a player who should score our first ever FA Cup goal,

then Nuge was that player. The one player who we know totally gets this thing of ours, the one player who if he wasn't out there playing for the red shirt, would be on the terraces supporting it. It was perfect, if you could script a football match you couldn't script it any better than that. The script got even better a few minutes later as Josh Howard slotted home a loose ball from a blocked Stuart Rudd overhead shot.

2-0 and the Road to Wembley (there's another!!) was looking smooth. Of course it wouldn't be a team in red called United if they didn't decide to make it a little more difficult, and with Trafford coming back into the game, before you knew it they had pulled it back to 2-2. Disbelief on most of the terrace, the songs seemed to get a little quieter and the nerves began to show, even at this early stage. Thankfully, FC started to pick their game back up and a Platt pen just before half time calmed the nerves a little to make it 3-2 at the break.

The second half was a scrappy affair, but thankfully FC were the better team and it looked only a matter of time that we would score again and give us a little breathing space. The fourth goal thankfully came courtesy of Simon Carden, after a cracking run down the left from Sheriff Shaun Roscoe, who was starting to make the left back position his own.

The goal relaxed everyone in the crowd a little, so much so that the section behind Sam Ashton's goal looked like the mosh pit at the Reading Festival. All you could see was bouncing bodies, crowd surfing, people on barriers and even a plastic mannequin leg being waved in the air. "We're on the march with Margy's army…." was sung over and over, and when they got bored with that "Follow follow follow, cause United are going to Fleetwood." It didn't rhyme, it didn't sound right, but it didn't matter, the intention was clear.

In my view the atmosphere so far this season hadn't been as good as in the past, but with the cup fever (three now!!) it had picked up and was back to its best. There was even time for sub Hargreaves to bundle in a fifth goal.

So onwards to Fleetwood in the next round......

Two days after the game, it was announced that Alex Mortimer had been released by the club. He had been in and out of the team due to the performances of Sheriff Roscoe during the first few games of the season and understandably wanted regular first team football. Alex had been the regular left back during the NWCL div 1 double winning campaign and always played with the full commitment we expect as fans of FC.

5th September 2007
Northern Premier Football League Challenge Cup: Round 1
FC United 0 Alsager Town 1 (after extra time)
Attendance: 867

It was time to begin the League Challenge Cup Trophy Thing campaign against Alsager at Radcliffe Borough's Stainton Park ground. It was a home game but due to the cost of hiring Gigg Lane for a game, and running the risk of losing money on a small crowd turning up, the correct decision was made to move the game. Personally I both like and loathe Radcliffe's ground. It has a pretty good club house and a few pubs within walking distance, which is always a bonus. It also felt a bit of a novelty at a home game being able to hear the players' shouts during the game. But there is no real scope for making a good atmosphere behind the goals, as behind one is a shallow seated stand, where you are in more danger of decapitation from flying footballs than singing yourself hoarse, and a small open terrace behind one goal. The only bit of covered standing is a little bus stop down the side, but due to some of the personnel that follow Alsager (well more their past exploits following a football league side) it was decided to segregate the crowd and they had the covered area.
I had been lurking on the Alsager forum for a couple of days previous to the game, to get an idea of how many would be making the trip. They saw it as quite a big game or them and had hired a coach and on that basis I would have expected maybe 50-100 fans, as it turned out, there were about 30 there. I had also noticed that one of them had been shopping for

something to bring to the game. I wondered if it would be inflatables, maybe old style rattles? Nope it was a batch of air horns. So the game sounded like a cross between a 80s East German European game, and a Manchester Storm (or whatever they are called these days) match. Still as long as the "Far side Ultras" were happy, who are we to complain? It at least brought some noise to the game, but after about 10 mins I have to be honest, it began to grate a little.

On the pitch, FC had two new boys playing in the shape of Liam George and Cayne Hanley. Both of these had been brought in during the start of the week, and not much was known about them. One had played for Burnley and the other had played for our brethren at AFC Wimbledon but beyond that, I had little clue.

The game itself was at best scrappy, Alsager starting the better, and forcing a couple of quality saves from Sam in goal, FC getting more into it and creating a few chances but they came to nothing. And so on the game went on……and on…….and on…….and on……and……well you get the picture.

I have to say the will to live was seeping out of me. The game in front of me was poor, the atmosphere was to say the least quiet (apart from the bloody air horns) and I was willing either keeper to throw the ball into the net so we could all go home, but 90 mins came and went with no goals, and so, with the game being decided on the night, we had the honour of 30 more minutes. Oh joy!

Extra time continued in the same vein, the game failing to liven up, with me sat behind the goal willing anyone to score, drop the ball in the net, give away a pen, anything to liven up the game basically.

Thankfully in the 109th minute (for all I knew it could have been the 4th day, it certainly felt like it!) Sam dropped the ball and after a scramble an Alsager player slotted the ball into the net. Cue pandemonium from the Alsager fans, and collective sigh of relief from people sat round me in the stand. FC continued to try and force penalties, which to be honest I had set myself up for and was secretly looking forward to, but alas it wasn't to be and

FC's run in this particular cup was ended at the first hurdle. Looking back, it's a shame really, as the next round would have been a home game with either Woodley or Curzon Ashton. Still, at least we can concentrate on the league, FA Cup, FA Trophy, President's Cup, Manchester Prem Cup, the Boat Race, the 100m Olympic final and the Grand National.

8th September 2007
FC United 2 (Carden 13, Patterson 52) Harrogate Railway 0
Attendance: 2196

Another busy pre match as 1600 tickets for the FA Cup game at Fleetwood were due to go on sale at the ticket office, as well as the U7s' Teddy Bears Picnic in the car park and the first couple of bands to play in the new initiative in Starkies at Gigg Lane, named by Brady "Course you can Malcolm" after the famous advert of the 1980s.

The club had decided to put tickets on sale to club members first for a couple of hours, then put them on open sale. This seemed fair as FC United is a members club, it is run by the members, for the members, it's one of the things that means we are different from the norm. Membership isn't required to attend a game of course, but it is for voting on club decisions and I agree with the decision to sell them to members when tickets are in short supply. Thankfully it didn't cause too much of a problem on the day, and come KO time, there were still a few hundred left.

One of the best things at FC is the amount of kids who come along to the games. As U16s aren't allowed to vote on club policy under IPS rules, the club has a junior supporters group, who meet once a month to provide something for the junior members to do. It has been mentioned in the past by various adult members, that very often the younger members seem to miss what is going on in these meetings, so a Teddy Bears picnic was organised, where they could play games, eat toffees and cakes, and dress up their bears for a comp to be judged by a couple of players.

On my regular trips out of the ticket office scrounging for change, I could see the kids were having a great time playing party games and dancing around. I must admit though I was worried when I saw them all sat on the floor in a line. I thought that of the organisers had decided enough was enough and had sat them all down to keep them quiet. Thankfully it was only so that Chaddy and Nicky Platt could judge the best dressed bear competition.

The game on the pitch was a 2-0 victory for FC. Harrogate looked a decent side, but couldn't make a breakthrough when the ball went up front. Carden opened the scoring with a close range overhead volley, and to be honest from then, the result never really looked in doubt. The second half brought much of the same, FC doing most of the pressing, Harrogate playing it about well until they got near the FC box and it just broke up.

Patterson made it 2-0 early on with a shot from the edge of the box and that was game over. Liam George was playing well wide on the right and with the news that Josh Howard could be out for a couple of months, cover on that side of the pitch will be vital.

The attendance was 2196, and most of them went home happy with 3 more points for FC.

After the game, we made our first visit of the season to the Swan and Cemetery for a pint. In the first season, this was the boozer of choice for most fans pre and post games, but a few issues occurred, resulting in most fans going elsewhere for refreshments. Personally, I have never really had any problems in there, the staff have always been fine with me, and they usually have a decent selection of pump ales on offer. It used to take ages to get served at the bar, but now it's just a gentle stroll up, get served and stroll back to the outside seating area to catch the last few rays of the late summer sun. They have even ditched the policy of serving in plastic as well. So it's a bravo from me for the Swan, a pub already etched into the history of the club.

11th September 2007
FC United 1(Patterson 37) Clitheroe 1 (abandoned after 58 min)
Attendance: 952

Speaking of places etched into the clubs history, Clitheroe FC was the venue of the next game. During the first season, FC played a friendly there on Easter Saturday. During this game, thanks to results elsewhere, the club were crowned NWCL div 2 champions. This sparked scenes of celebration on the pitch at the end of the game, and in The Bridge pub next to the ground. It also saw Phil Power get the life mithered out of him in a pub in Astley later on that night.

With all this in mind a crowd of just fewer than 1,000 gathered on a warm Wednesday night to see if FC could continue their winning run or Clitheroe could pick up their first win of the season.

For the majority of the first half, it looked like the latter, as Clitheroe did most of the attacking and had the clearer of the chances, so it was a surprise when Rory found himself some space in the box for probably the first time in the game and rifled the ball home. Sadly this didn't spur FC on as the majority of the crowd would have hoped and Clitheroe continued to press the FC defence and it was no surprise when they equalised just before half time.

The second half started as scrappily as the first ended with neither side putting a maker down on the game. Then, after about 15 mins, something unique in my footballing life occurred. The ball ran out of play in front of the main stand and then plink, the lights went out. Well, one light on each floodlight remained on, but ¾ of the pitch were shrouded in darkness. This led to 10 minutes of confusion before it became apparent that the game couldn't continue and the ref had to call the game off.

The talk on the way out was of how long does the game have to be before it is classed as a game and the result can stand, will there have to be a replay and if so, how much will admission be

and will Stuart Rudd still be suspended for the FA Cup game at Fleetwood?
The day after brought some quite frankly ridiculous views from some FC fans, that for some reason Clitheroe had turned the lights off on purpose in an attempt to make money for a second time. These claims were rejected later that day in a statement from the Clitheroe club which said that they were making a donation of £1000 to the FC Development Fund, charging £4 for adults and £2 for concessions for the rearranged fixture, and would be giving the first 500 people through the turnstiles a free programme. The statement also made a point of commending the fans for their conduct in leaving the ground, and also made a comment on the great relationship that existed between the two clubs. Hardly the behaviour of a club out to make a quick buck if we are honest.

15th September 2007
FA Cup: 1st Qualifying Round
Fleetwood Town 2 FC United 1 (Patterson 25)
Attendance: 3112

Ever since the win at Trafford, the game at Fleetwood had been at the forefront of most people's minds. During the days leading up to the game the finding of a decent pub was planned. The pre-requisites being nice ales, a boozer quiet enough to sit down and a place decent for smoking. The Prince Albert was suggested, due to its real ales, but a quick internet search discovered the place had a picture of Anfield on the wall, and also with the dippers on Sky, it was thought that it probably wasn't the best place to go. Another search found the North Euston Hotel on the "promenade" at Fleetwood. It was a regular in the good beer guide and so that was decided on.
The day started with an early arrival at Piccadilly Station in time for the 9.11 to Blackpool North. After the customary visit to Smiths for provisions we trooped off to platform 14 to wait for the train. We were greeted at the entrance of the platform with a line of hectors, and behind them, police. I made a comment that

it was a touch of overkill for people going to a non-league football match miles away, and this was even more evident on getting to the platform and seeing about another five members of GMP. Of course I had forgotten that the Liverpool Lime St train also leaves from this platform and with MUFC playing at Everton at 12 noon, the police were actually there to keep a watchful eye on the people catching that train. The train to Lime Street left the platform around five mins before the Blackpool one, and it was funny to see the reaction of the police after it had left with the platform still full of people wearing red scarves.

On arrival at Blackpool, we took a gentle stroll down to the North Pier to await a tram to take us to Fleetwood and our pre-game hostelry of choice.

As expected, the North Euston was quiet, though there was more FC'ers in there than I thought there would be, the ale was as good as expected and a few beers were taken sat outside the hotel in the late summer Fleetwood sun.

We arrived at the ground at about 14.35 to find a short queue outside the away turnstiles. My first thoughts were that we would be lucky to get the game started at 3 o'clock. This proved to be correct, but sadly not just because of crowd congestion. Once we got through the queue and into the ground, the first thing I noticed was the players were warming up in blue shorts and so finally the 3rd kit would make an appearance.

We took our place in the stand and heard the expected announcement that the kick off was to be put back ten minutes to allow the crowds to come in. It was shortly after this that I noticed Sam Ashton lying flat out on the floor. It was obvious that he had been hit by something thrown from behind the goal. I could see the home fans were gesticulating towards the corner where the FC fans were still coming in and on mooching down to the corner I found that the FC fans were reacting to this incident. There was lots of shouting, finger pointing and general anger towards the Fleetwood fans, as more missiles were thrown onto the pitch. At this point, Ashton fell again and the referee had no option but to take the players off the pitch. An announcement was made that if this was to continue the game

would be called off. This seemed to calm the mood down on either side of the temporary segregation, and thankfully, 20 minutes or so late, the game started.
The delay seemed to affect FC more as Fleetwood started the brighter of the two teams. They pressed the harder and forced a couple of saves out of a recovered Ashton. The best chance early on though fell to Patterson who managed to twist his way through the Fleetwood defence, lose a boot and force a decent save from the keeper. It was a shame the ball didn't go in, I had visions of a new verse being added to his song. "He scores with one boot" indeed.
The game exploded into life on 18 mins, when one of the Fleetwood players fell over in the box after what appeared to be the most minimal of contact. The ref pointed to the spot and the pen was slotted into the corner of the net. So not the best start for FC but there was time for us to get back into the game, and it took only seven minutes for Patterson to get us back on level terms.
This was the score at half time, and the second half started just as the first one did with Fleetwood doing most of the attacking and Ashton keeping them at bay with a couple of decent saves.
The game was getting more and more niggly, with tackles flying in and one Fleetwood player escaping with only a yellow card after raising his hands off the ball to Jerome Wright.
The assistant on the far side of the pitch was also getting very involved in the game by seeming to give every little bit of contact by a FC player as a foul, and infuriating the FC fans massed behind the goal.
The odds seemed to move into favour of FC as the same said assistant spotted an off the ball incident and after a discussion, the ref produced the red card. I hope Nuge managed to get all the spittle off his face.
The FC fans in the 3112 crowd hoped that this would spur the lads on to victory, but they hadn't allowed for yet another intervention from the assistant, who adjudged Sheriff Roscoe had pulled down a Fleetwood attacker in the box. From my vantage point in the stand, it looked like he got a very large

chunk of the ball and that another soft penalty had been given. The penalty was again slotted into the net.
FC fought hard to get back into the game and had plenty of possession but the final ball was lacking more often than not.
As the game neared the final whistle, FC had one final push with Patterson and Platt both making the Fleetwood keeper work hard to keep the ball out of the net but sadly the game ended 2-1 to Fleetwood and the road to Wembley in the FA Cup was over.
It has to be said at this point that as the Fleetwood players and the match official were leaving the field, some of our supporters didn't cover themselves in too much glory by abusing and spitting at them. Though to put this into context, and without trying to excuse the behaviour, football is an emotional sport and at times these emotions can run over which is what seems to have occurred at the end of the game. Unlike other events, it can't be said this was pre-meditated and planned.
Outside the ground the inevitable skirmishes were going on, it was almost like coming out of WBA or Leicester back in the day.
We walked back into Fleetwood, enjoying the delights of the Fleetwood "mob" playing cat and mouse with the local constabulary and shouting abuse at us, and straight to the North Euston for a few post match drinks and the tram back into Blackpool through the illuminations in time for the 21.50 train back to Blighty.
The main issue of the day was the missile throwing at Sam Ashton and how it could have been stopped. I believe it could have been prevented by having more stewards at that end and at least a couple of policemen in the ground. This would have acted as a deterrent to anyone intent on causing trouble. Instead the police seemed happier outside the FC turnstiles, filming fans of a non-league football club as they entered a non-league ground.
The problem with bringing the police into the ground, it would seem, is the fact that as soon as they take one foot in the ground, a bill appears in the post to the home club. This of course would

affect the profit of the home club but it's my opinion that the safety of the fans and players in the ground comes before the pile of pounds. This isn't just an issue at Fleetwood, it has happened at many grounds before and probably will as we move up the ladder.

22nd September 2007
FC United 1 (Patterson 44) Woodley Sports 1
Attendance: 2283

As we all know it took MUFC 26 years to win the title, but spare a thought for those of us who also follow Lancashire County Cricket Club. The last time they won the championship outright was in 1934, all of 73 years ago. Finally in 2007 the title was in touching distance. I had been watching Lancashire since 1988 and for the first time in my lifetime, going into the last game of the season the title was there to be won. Lancs were in top spot and just needed a win to secure the title. With this in mind, I decided to give the game against Woodley a swerve to travel down to The Oval to see if Lancs could do it. I was kept informed of happenings at Gigg, and was hoping for a positive result in both games. Sadly I was in for disappointment.
Despite needing a record run chase to win the game and the title, Lancashire got oh so close, in the end missing out by 25 runs, in a game which made the 3 FC'ers in the Oval crowd as proud as they had been over many years watching MUFC and FC. It was like 1992 all over again. My team had led the table all season only to fall short right at the end. Sussex to Leeds United, Chris Adams to Gordon Strachan. How I hate those men for doing what they did to me.
Meanwhile at Gigg, FC were drawing 1-1 with Woodley, Rory scoring the equaliser after Woodley had taken an early lead.
In the days following the game, the unofficial internet forum was red hot with observations about the game, how poor it was, the performance not up to scratch, the crowd very quiet and so on. Not being at the game I couldn't comment on the

performance, but reading the views expressed both heartened and worried me in equal measures.

It was good to read that the fans care enough about the club and team that poor performances got the blood boiling and people hot under the collar. It also seemed to me a sign of how far we had come, that we had a team and club that had set such high standards in the previous two seasons, and a blip in performance was such a cause for concern.

It also worried me though. One of the most oft repeated mantras over the previous seasons had been that FC is a broad church. People come at it from different angles, for some it's a protest purely against the Glazer regime at M16, for others it's a strike back at what professional football has become and for some it's just a day on the beer with a football match at some point. I sensed in the days following the game, from some of the comments aired, that the idea of charging up the league was important, promotion this season is vital and on current performance that wouldn't be achieved. It was said that the club could be in danger of standing still. The club can't stand still, we need to continue to grow and improve and build towards a future but it would be a shame in my view if the events on the field became the be all and end all of FC United. It is important of course, that is what we pay our money to go and watch of a weekend, but FC is so much more than that.

Every time the team takes to the pitch and plays a game it is a protest against the events of 2005 at Old Trafford, every time a fan buys a season ticket and pays admission to a game, it is a protest to the Glazers and the direction of professional football in general. Every time the club holds a members meeting and vote, it is showing that fans can have a say in how a football club is run and that is without even mentioning the community and schools projects that the club has been involved in over the past couple of years.

It would be a shame if the club progressed so far and what happens on the pitch becomes all that FC United is about, with some of the core principles left behind in the grand pursuit for total success. There needs to be a balance, to be able to show that a club can be run by its fans, be visible in the community and be successful on the pitch, but it needs to be remembered that all those aren't mutually exclusive and each one is just as important as the others.

29th September 2007
Chorley FC 0 FC United 3 (Rudd 13, Patterson 37 62)
Attendance: 1736

During the first two seasons, days out to Chorley have been most enjoyable. This has been mainly due to the ease with which you can get there, plenty of pubs in the town and a large and welcoming clubhouse in the ground. On the two occasions the games were against Daisy Hill and Atherton LR, games moved thanks to their own grounds not being able to hold the crowd. Finally though this season, we got to play Chorley in their own ground, with all the delights the town has to offer (did I really just use the words Chorley and delights in the same sentence?)
The day started off with a splendid breakfast in the FC friendly Koffee Pot in Manchester. For four for your hard earned you get a freshly cooked breakfast, a pile of toast that could rival the tower in Pisa and a cup of fair-trade tea. Couple this with a nice bohemian atmosphere and you have the perfect start to the FC away day.
We jumped on the 12.11 rattler which was heaving with people on their way to Blackpool, a mother and daughter who were going out for a night on the lash in said seaside town and a couple of wannabes who complained loudly that "….they've taken our seats." Now far be it for me to point this out but they were in standard class on a cattle wagon going to Blackpool, how did they have seats of their own?
Anyway, as usual on arrival it was a short wander into the Chorley clubhouse to get a quiet ale before it became taters deep and after a chat with Wayne, the intrepid Non League Paper reporter and a purchase of the development fund badge, we took

our place in the stand, which this season seems to have become the vantage point of choice.

Matters on the pitch didn't get off to a great start as Browny pulled his back in the warm up which meant Margy had some shuffling about to do. Spenner was moved into the back four and The Power took his place on the bench.

Since starting to sit in the stands at away games, I have noticed the amount of local kids that are at our games. Now this you would have thought would be a good thing, but sadly they are usually of the sort that wear trackie bottoms tucked in Simpsons socks. They also seem to turn up with an attitude of aggression, albeit just from the mouth, towards the FC fans and team. Still at least the home clubs are getting some extra gate money and of course if they are in the ground watching the match, there are some grannies out on the street getting their pensions home safely.

The game started as most others, the home team having a good amount of the ball and FC looking dangerous going forward. The Chorley No 7 on the right wing was seeing lots of the ball but thankfully seemed to run out of steam when he got anywhere near the FC box.

Stuart Rudd fired FC into the lead and from that point the game was pretty much over. Chorley just seemed to let their heads collectively drop as FC pretty much saw all of the ball and should have gone two up when new boy Adam Carden went through on the right but fired his shot at the keeper.

One thing that was obvious in the first half was how good a player Chris Baguley will be for FC. Since he signed in pre-season, he has struggled to keep himself fit and so hasn't had a run in the team but when he has played, he has impressed on every occasion with his vision, knack of seemingly being able to find space anywhere on the pitch and his shooting, which he proved with a freekick that curled onto the crossbar. It's certainly an area that FC are well off in with Baguley, Spencer, Platt and Si Carden vying for the two central spots.

Chorley tried their best to make a game of it, especially the Paul Kitson look-alike up front but Rory scored to make it two nil and the game was pretty much over before half time.

During the half time break we saw yet more inept policing at a FC game. At games where it has been possible and as is customary at non league level, the fans have at half time made their way round to stand behind the goal FC are attacking in the second half. This isn't exclusive to FC and certainly wasn't brought in at the formation of the club, it has happened since time immemorial; fans are free to walk round the perimeter of the pitch as they wish to. Not so it seems at Chorley despite the fact that during the Daisy Hill and Atherton games previous, it wasn't a problem.

Before the game it was announced there would be "light segregation" whatever that may entail, surely segregation is there or isn't and there was certainly no mention that fans couldn't change ends. Sadly, as the FC lot made their way to the opposite end of the ground, they were met by a cordon of police who stopped them from going any further. This resulted in a bit of a stand off and the inevitable climb over the barriers to walk past the police. Should this have happened? Well maybe not, but in the face of such over the top jobsworthiness, it seemed fair enough. This resulted in the police forming a line at the side of the small roofed terrace and making the FC fans who had gathered in there leave and stand on the grass bank at the side.

We were then left with the ridiculous sight of an empty terrace as the Chorley fans had been allowed to go to the opposite end of the ground, and a good number of FC stood on a grassy bank with a line of the local constabulary stopping them going any further. It was farcical and if you didn't laugh at it, you would probably cry at the stupidity on show. Finally, a message seemed to be sent out to the police and common sense was seen with the police line moving and allowing the FC lot into the stand.

It was like Fleetwood in reverse, when police were needed they were nowhere to be seen but on a ground where we have played

twice before with no hint of trouble a police presence akin to The Who on tour in the 70s is on show.
With about 30 mins to go Patterson scored from a cross from Wright to end the game and spark off a celebratory atmosphere behind the goal with the fans singing and bouncing up and down.
After the game, we wandered up into Chorley to find a quiet pub that was showing the Birmingham V MUFC game, which we found in The George just off the main street.
The day after the Chorley game, the U18 side played a cup game against Bury Amateurs on Albert Park in Salford. We got there just after half time, with FC leading 2-1. The second half was entertaining, with the stronger and more physical Bury side equalising to take the game into extra time. Within a few minutes of extra time kicking off, the game was pretty much over as FC had scored 2 quick goals to run out 4-2 winners.
There are some good players to look out for in the U18s side, it is fair to say they all show promise and if they come through as we would like, the future of the club is very bright indeed.

October 2007

2nd October 2007
Skelmersdale United 3 FC United 1(Patterson 17)
Attendance: 617

Skelmersdale on a Tuesday night was always going to be a problem. Thanks to the attitude of one of their club officials last season when the Formby game was moved there, blaming FC United for setting the bench mark for £7 admission charges as well as MUFC being at home to Roma live on ITV, it was always going to be a small crowd. The lowest competitive crowd so far proved this, and sadly as it turned out, the ones that sat it out probably did the best thing.

The game started with FC looking like a team that hadn't seen each other before, never mind played together. The defence were looking like four strangers, and whilst the team looked ok going forward it was no surprise that Skem took the lead with a shot slammed the ball into the roof of the net. The home team certainly were the better side and looked dangerous when from out of nothing Rory pulled out another one of his wonder goals, this time a moving, swerving, dipping shot from about 35 yards that flew into the top corner. One all and game on.

Rory forced the keeper to make a couple of decent saves and was also stamped on by a defender, something both the ref and linesman missed, despite all the crowd on the second grassy knoll of the week seeing it. In fact it is surprising the ref actually gave any decisions at all as he seemed far more interested in trying to coach the two teams. All night he seemed to be saying to the teams "No foul" when the ball was coming to a player and "Well done you two, keep going" etc etc. I think if he had been concentrating on doing his job, he would have seen some of the fouls that occurred.

It was also interesting to notice that for the first time this season neither team had a sponsor on the front of their shirts.

I am not sure what Margy said at half time, but sadly it didn't seem to have any effect as it seemed we had been taken back in time to when films were silent. The defence had been replaced by the Keystone Cops and I am sure I saw Charlie Chaplin,

Harold Lloyd and Laurel and Hardy out on the pitch at various points of the second half. To say the performance was disappointing would be an understatement. It was no surprise when Skem cut through the FC defence again and Evans side-footed the ball into the net to make it 2-1.
FC huffed and puffed but it just wasn't clicking, too many players having off nights all at the same time and no decent service to Rudd and Patterson. It was sad to see and hear how frustrated Rory was for most of the second half.
There were half chances; Si Carden headed onto the roof of the net, Rory hit a free kick over the bar, Rudd had a header kicked off the line, but if the truth be told Sam Ashton was keeping FC in the game with a number of decent saves.
The ref added 5 mins injury time but to be honest if he added on 5 days it wouldn't have made any difference. To add insult to injury, Skem added a third with Evans completing his hat trick. Not a good night at the office and it left Margy and the fans with plenty to think about going into the tough FA Trophy game at Bradford Park Avenue.

Two nights after the Skem debacle was the monthly FC United Development Fund meeting. These open monthly meetings were set up to focus attention on the importance of the development fund and the need to raise money to build our own ground as soon as is humanly possible.
Gigg Lane has been useful to the club for the past couple of years in terms of its size and proximity to motorway, regular bus service and a tram line, but financial requirements to play there mean that it can't really be considered a long term tenancy and plans need to be put in place to raise the funds towards a home to call our own. At the start of the season, it was decided to hold monthly open meetings where all supporters could attend and put forward ideas on money raising, get updates on how the fund is going, what we need to do to get there and what the club are doing to reach the goal.
A four man committee of Martin Morris from the FC board, Vinny Thompson, George Hayden and Gary Selvidge was

formed to help co-ordinate this. The meetings are an open forum for all fans to share ideas and pool skills and strengths.
At the first DF meeting, it was decided that a target of £500K was to be raised by the fans and the first £100K of this to be raised by the end of season 2007-08. It was a tough target to hit but fans got onto raising money in many ways. The juniors' organised activities on match days, fans signed up for sponsored bike rides across the country, a draw which would allow the winning fan to become a fully registered member of the playing squad was set up and of course the writing of books such as the one you are reading.
At the October meeting there were around 32 people in attendance, which isn't bad going for a Thursday night, but sadly it was pretty much the same faces that attend each meeting. Of course there are many willing hands that can't get down to the meetings and who do get involved, but it would be nice to see some new blood down at the meetings.

It's always good to come across fans outside FC that "get it." By that I mean fans who understand the club and all that it is about and stands for. One such set of fans are the guys at Mudhuts Media who follow Wigan Athletic. Their path mirrors the one we are taking, they started in non league and ended up in the Premiership and all that entails. They started up the first ever Wigan fanzine "Cockney Latic" which was a newsletter aimed at London based Wiganers and are responsible for a fanzine called Mudhutter Football Express and a multi media website featuring a forum, podcasts, T-shirts etc. They also have written a couple of books, one of which "Pies and Prejudice" was a diary of their season where they were finally promoted from Div 1 or whatever it is called this week, to the Prem. A very good read it is too. Anyway, a few of us were invited down to The Brickmakers Pub in Wigan for the launch of their new book "Punk Football" written by Andrew Vaughan, which tells the story of the 1977 season when Wigan were in the Northern Premier League and punk was starting to take hold around the country.

It was the first time I had met these guys, and what sound chaps they turned out to be, knowledgeable on football, music and refreshingly FC. We chatted about FC, the game at Old Trafford the day after when MUFC were at home to Wigan, their impending visit to Gigg Lane and "Course you Can Malcolm" and we scoffed some quality pie and peas. It was also good to see their book sales skills were as good as our very own Brady's as they had to be asked number of times if we could buy a copy of the book.

6th October 2007
FA Trophy Preliminary Round
Bradford Park Avenue 1 FC United 1 (Patterson 54)
Attendance: 1310

The second Road to Wembley in The FA Trophy saw us with a trip over the Pennines to play the famous Bradford Park Avenue at the Horsfall Stadium.

An early trip over meant we were sat in the Kings Head near the ground nice and early for the MUFC v Wigan game on tele. A 4-0 win later and we were off to the ground to sample a very poor pie, but made up for slightly with some decent peas and mint gravy. A nice twist I thought and one that others should copy. It also has to be said that it was a very strange ground with a running track round the pitch, a cricket type pavilion along the side that housed the dressing rooms. It was a strange mish mash of things, but they all added up to a ground with character.

As the teams took the field, the familiar strains of Gerry Marsden were played over the tannoy. No doubt the conspiracy theorists were foaming at the mouth and thinking that it was being played solely for our benefit, but on investigation with a Bradford fan sat behind me I was assured they always play this. He also told me that they used to play Electric Avenue by Eddy Grant, so I suppose it is from the bad to the downright awful.

FC made a very bright start to the game as if to attempt to shake off the cobwebs of the poor show the previous Tuesday. In a mirror image of the MUFC game, FC had to make two changes due to injuries to Adam Carden and Stu Rudd inside the first

half an hour. Happily this didn't seem to upset the rhythm of the team, as substitute Hanley brought a save from the Bradford keeper.
Despite the announcements that standing wasn't allowed in the seats, the vocal element of the FC following made their home at the end of the stand and were in very fine voice. Half time was reached with the game goal-less but with a FC performance that was 1000 times better than the one at Skem.
The second half started pretty much as the first ended with FC on top, Patterson firing just wide. It was shortly after this when one of the most bizarre moments of the season happened. As we were watching the game, a pair of pink ladies pants appeared on the corner of the FC dugout. After a little bit of digging, it transpired that this was a challenge set by a couple of regular Boogie Bus travellers, who decided to take the pants from the washing line, and return them later in the season when we played the league game there.
Back to the pitch and Nicky Platt had a shot kicked off the line shortly before Hanley played Patterson in who finished in his usual way and it was 1-0 to FC. This seemed to spur PA on, and they forced the first save of the game from Sam Ashton with the rebound thankfully being put wide.
Sadly, the lead couldn't last, as a long ball forward resulted in Chaddy, a PA attacker and Ashton all challenging for the ball. It seemed like Ashton had been fouled as he jumped and dropped the ball and as the crowd all waited for the ref's whistle the ball was forced into the net via the Sheriff on the line and also the post. Despite the claims from some of the FC players the goal stood, and this brought a tense final few minutes as PA started to play, and they forced a fine double save from Ashton to keep us in the Trophy.
The game ended 1-1 with the first ever replay in FC's short history taking place on the following Wednesday.
During the second half, and for reasons not entirely clear, a collection of "security staff" gathered on the running track at the front of the FC fans. There had been no trouble and no hint of trouble and so it does beg the question why this show of strength

was needed. It did seem that a missile of some sort did land on the pitch, but this was from outside the ground and from nowhere near the FC fans. Of course all this meant was that there was a bit of antagonism shown from the fans towards the bouncers stood in front of them. All totally unnecessary to be honest.

After the game we headed into Bradford to sample one of their famous curries. We decided on the Karachi as it had good reviews on tinterweb and also from Rick Stein. It was a strange place, like having a meal in a cross between a shop and someone's front room. The food was ok, had worse but certainly had better. I made a mental note to have a rethink for the game later on in the season.

10th October 2007
FA Trophy Preliminary Round, Replay
FC United 1 (Hanley 85) Bradford Park Avenue 4
Attendance: 951

The replay took place the following Wednesday. None of this needing over a weeks notice that has crept into professional football in the past 15 years or so, draw on a Sat get the tie over and done with that week. Just as it should be. The game was played at Radcliffe due to the club not being too sure of how many would attend and of course the cost of holding extra games at Gigg. The fans gathered in the bus stop down the side were in fine voice and with a good performance in the original game confidence was high. Well it was until the match started.

FC began quite brightly, Patterson had a free kick go close and Bradford had a couple of chances wide, but on 13 minutes a defensive mix up allowed Bradford to take the lead as Gedman pounced to slot the ball into an empty net. It didn't get much better as just before the half hour, Bradford sprung the offside trap for the umpteenth time and made it 2-0.

Those two goals made for a poor first half after a decent opening from FC.

Bradford started the second half as they finished the first, on top and it came as no surprise when the broke down the left again and it was 3-0. It seemed that Bradford came with a definite game plan to use the left wing and it was working as Liam Foster was being attacked incessantly.
Margy made a double change at this point by bringing off both Foster and Sheriff Roscoe and bringing on attacking players to try and force a way back into the game. The lads did start to play, but with only three at the back and with the attacking intentions of Bradford, it seemed inevitable that Bradford would get a fourth. They did.
FC did force a reply from Hanley late on but it was to no avail and FC suffered a poor defeat to, if we are being honest, a good team who played the perfect game on the break.
So the second Road to Wembley was over and the poor run in national cup competitions continued. Ahh well, Wembley looks like an airport anyway.

13th October 2007
FC United 2 (Baguley 60 81) Wakefield 1
Attendance: 1955

As has been the norm at home games this season so far, I had to open the ticket office to see if we could drum up some business for the away cup game at Droylsden but before that I got the chance for a beer in "Course you can Malcolm" with the Mudhuts Media Wigan lads who had come down for the game, and to grab an interview with Vaughanie, who wrote "Punk Football", for a forthcoming issue of Under the Boardwalk.
After the interview and surprisingly brisk sales at the ticket office it was time to actually see a Gigg Lane kick off for once as I managed to get into the ground just before 3 o'clock.
The game started well, with FC starting brightly but more importantly the crowd getting right behind the team. I hadn't been at the previous home league game, but one of the complaints had been that the crowd had been a little quiet compared to how it usually was. It was obviously that these

comments had been taken on board as the singing was at its usual volume and was non stop pretty much throughout the game.

The one black spot on the first half was the injury to Chaddy which he received from a late tackle. As he was helped off it looked quite bad and that was proven after the game with the news that he would be missing for quite a few weeks.

Half time came with the score goal-less, FC having a few chances but the flow being interrupted by the constant shrill of the referee's whistle with his finger pointing mostly in favour of the away team. This seems to be a common thread to this season so far.

The second half started as the first finished, FC having most of the ball but struggling to keep hold of it. As usual Rory Patterson was all over the pitch getting involved back in midfield, chasing lost causes and generally getting up the noses of the Wakefield players, all the things that Rory does best.

The deadlock was broken with a fantastic Chris Baguley free kick which curled into the top corner. Since he signed it was clear what a great shot he had, and it was good to see this in action for his first FC goal. Sadly the lead only lasted four minutes as Wakefield broke through the middle of the FC defence and equalised.

This was hopefully the kick for FC to go on and get a winner but it was Wakefield who looked the most likely and hit the post with an over head kick. This did spur FC who took the game by the scruff of the neck and with nine minutes to go Baguley repeated his first goal with another free kick from the same position into the same part of the net.

FC had got the show back on the road with a tough win in front of a slightly disappointing crowd of just over 1900. Hopefully this was due to the day of television sport and the poor weather and not a vision of how crowds would be averaging themselves out.

16th October 2007
Clitheroe 0 FC United 3 (Burns 6 66, Patterson 55 pen)
Attendance: 834

In true non league fashion, the games kept on coming as midweek brought another trip to the hills of Clitheroe. This was the rearranged game thanks to the floodlight failure a few weeks earlier. The traffic from town getting to the game was horrendous but after a detour that took in Salford, Cheetham Hill, Crumpsall, Moston and Ramsbottom, I finally made it to Clitheroe.

The home club were true to their word of only charging four quid in and a free programme to the first 500 people through the gates, a fine gesture made by a friendly club.

The game also marked the debut of Aaron Burns for FC. He had been signed a few days earlier to fill the gap made by the injury to Stuart Rudd. Burns had played for MUFC reserves in the previous season and was going to sign for Cardiff. He had found his path to the first team blocked by the signings of Hasselbaink and Fowler and so decided to seek football elsewhere. He was unable to sign for a club above Unibond standard before January and so he was at FC for a few months.

It only took Burns six minutes to open his FC account with a tap in from a cross by Wright who had rounded the keeper. It was clear to anyone in the ground the class Burns had, his touch and movement was head and shoulders above anyone else on the pitch and this seemed to bring out the best in some of his team mates as Jerome Wright was having the best game he had had for some weeks.

The chances were flowing for FC, Nugent headed a free header wide from a corner and Wright forced a great save from the home keeper.

Early in the second half, Patterson forced his way into the box only to be brought down, the ref having no doubt in pointing to the spot. Patterson dusted himself down and in the absence of usual taker Platt, slotted the penalty into the net to put FC two goals up. At this point I have to ask are there any other people in life who "dust themselves down" before doing something. It seems a very strange phrase to use. At no point did I see Rory get up from the floor, rub his fingers down his chest and a cloud of dust evaporate into the air.

There were a few nervous glances round the ground and comments made regarding how long the floodlights would last this time, thankfully they lasted the distance and Burns wrapped up the win with a cool clinical finish into the net after a superb run and cross from the right set him up.

A very respectable crowd of 834 was there to see this FC win, a win that put the club into 4th position in the league. It also emerged during the game, that FC had made another signing, a player by the name of Colin Bell. At first it seemed that Margy had lost his marbles, bringing in a crocked ex bitter in his 60s, but thankfully it turned out to be a "utility" player from Carmarthen who has a fine red pedigree.

20th October
Man ciddy U17s 3 FC United 3 (Platt (pen), Thomson, Patterson)
Attendance 38

The defeat to Bradford meant that FC had a free weekend after the game at Clitheroe. The reserves had a game but I quite fancied a weekend off from football, save watching MUFC on the tele in the pub. I quite fancied it, but it didn't end up that way.

I turned my phone on only for it to bleep straight away with a message from the club sec to say the first team had a friendly at Platt Lane against the U17 side of Man City and I was welcome to attend. I didn't need asking again and I jumped into the car and shot straight down.

On arrival at Platt Lane, George the Kitman saw me and came straight over to find out how I knew about the game. I told him that I had been invited and there had been no "leak" so all was ok.

The team lined up with Theo Coleman on the left wing, Jerome at left back, Colin Bell in the centre of defence alongside the Sheriff with Aaron Burns up front with Rory. On the bench was another new signing Peter Thomson, who actually looked like two players glued together.
The game started brightly with both teams looking to attack. As it was pretty much a training match there was acres of space for both teams to play in and this resulted in some good attacking play.
FC took the lead with a soft penalty after a foul on Liam Foster. Nicky Platt fired the penalty into the net but not before some classic bitterness from a resident div stood beside me.
"Come on ref that was never a pen." Which he may have had a point with but with the immortal line "You are just biased ref" it proved that even when the ciddy youth team are playing a non league team the bitterness seeps out and knows no bounds.
Half time came with FC still one up but it had been a good game, ciddy actually have a cracking team at this age group, very fast and skilful. Margy made a couple of changes at half time, bringing on Thomson and Hanley and straight away Thomson made a nuisance of himself. He scored soon after coming on to make it 2-0. I would love to describe a beautiful flowing move to you, how the ball broke from defence, went through 8 players and flew into the top corner of the net from Thomson's boot. I would love to, but sadly due to turning away to speak for a split second, I missed the goal.
Soon after it was 2-1, ciddy hit the bar, then 2-2. At this point it looked like FC had gone. Due to their age and the fact they train every day the ciddy team were looking much fitter and were the most likely team to go on and win. Course Mr Patterson had something to say about that as he lobbed the blue keeper from outside the box to put FC 3-2 back in the lead. A lead that was to last just a few minutes before a quality ciddy goal made the game 3-3 and that is how it stayed until full time. A crowd of 38 saw a decent game of football played in the right spirit.
After the game had finished, and in the car about to leave my phone rang. It was Brady.

"Where are you?"
"I am just about to leave, why?"
"Don't run off, you can help us with a job."
The first thing that crossed my mind is that there was some top secret scran laid on to eat somewhere in Platt Lane. Alas it turned out that I was required to help Walshy, Brady and Lindsey in B&Q buying and carrying stuff for kitting out the new offices.
One of the reasons that FC United was set up was to avoid the possibility of spending Saturday afternoons traipsing round B&Q, but here I was doing it on behalf of the club. You really couldn't make it up.

23rd October 2007
Manchester Premier Cup: Round 1
Droylsden FC 2 FC United 3 (Hanley 12, Burns 58, Patterson 60)
Attendance: 1048

The following midweek brought yet another cup competition in the guise of the Manchester Premier Cup, a competition for non league teams affiliated to the Manchester FA. The draw paired us with Droylsden from the Conference at The Butcher's Arms, a ground that was close to being home for FC in its early days.
In the run up to this game there had been upset that Droylsden were charging £10 to attend the game. This may have seemed high but it needed to be considered that it was actually a reduction on their usual admission. There was also a fear that both teams would field reserve sides with priorities elsewhere for both clubs, but FC put out their strongest side and on inspection of the official team sheet and comparing it to previous line ups, the Droylsden side was pretty strong, all their players having Conference experience including a certain Jamie Tandy who was the recipient a couple of Christmases ago of a cigar from Joey Barton as his present. Sadly it was placed in his eye and not his hand.

It has started to become a habit at away games to sit in the stand for the matches. It makes it a little easier to see the game with writing in mind and you usually have a good laugh with the home fans. But not at The Butcher's it would seem.
Just as the teams were about to kick off, a shout came from our left, "Come on Bloods beat this shower of shit, hammer the pretenders." This brought a few raised eyebrows and stifled laughter from the FC'ers sat in hearing distance of the "lady."
On being asked if she could sit back as "The chip on her shoulder was getting in the way of me seeing the game," she began a tirade of bitterness that would have been at home a few miles up the road at Wastelands.
"I have been a season ticket holder at Old Trafford for 40 odd years, who do you think you are?" came the reply back. A quick laugh and shake of the head soon saw that come to a close and minds turned to matters on the pitch.
Droylsden started pretty strongly as you would expect, with the FC goal leading a charmed life at times. The ball was kicked off the FC line twice in the space of seconds as FC seemed to be struggling to handle the speed of the forward line.
The game was bitty as both teams were caught offside time after time and with a picky ref who never actually left a 10 yard area around the centre circle and seemed to be working on some sort of satellite delay when making decisions.
On 12 minutes Cayne Hanley put FC ahead with a header but at the other end, Droylsden were still causing a few problems and a great save from Sam Ashton kept the game at 1-0. The game started to open up, with FC looking dangerous on the counter attack and coming close on a few occasions, with the keeper making a number of decent saves.
The second half started similar to the first with both teams looking to attack but without actually playing much football. This was until Nicky Platt played a great ball forward to Aaron Burns, who controlled the ball and fired a powerful shot past the Droylsden keeper and onto the inside of the far post, before dropping into the net for two nil. A couple of minutes later it got even better as a break down the right saw the ball cut back for

Patterson to roll the ball into the net for 3-0. A quick look to our left saw the loudmouth Bloods fan with her head in her hands and the sound of laughter in her ears. “Not bad for a shower of shit” I think was also heard.
As expected the home side started to come back into the game and a great finish saw them pull a goal back, but despite a few scares the FC defence was holding pretty well especially Rob Nugent who seemed to be getting in the way of everything.
In the last minute though panic started to set in as the ref, for some reason, saw a foul in the FC box and pointed straight to the spot. The penalty was slotted home and it made for a hairy last few minutes of injury time but FC held out to claim a great victory and a home against Flixton Fc in the next round.

27th October 2007
FC United 3 (Patterson 39 66, Thompson 90) Ossett Albion 1
Attendance: 2160

After the giant killing it was back to league action with the visit of Ossett Albion to Gigg Lane. Pre match I was looking after the ticket office with match tickets, club Christmas party tickets and tickets to a Leigh Branch race night for the Development Fund all on sale. I was also dishing out the newly printed members' yearbook so as usual it was a bit busy.
I got into Gigg Lane at just gone 3pm to see that we were one down already, yet another goal missed by yours truly.
Margy had kept faith with the same starting XI as the previous Tuesday and had new signings Jamie Baguley and Peter Thomson on the bench.
The first half was quite an even affair with not much goal action, FC doing most of the attacking and putting in many crosses but with no one on the end of them. It took until the 39th minute when a parry off the keeper from a Chris Baguley shot hit Mr Patterson and dropped into the net. FC deservedly on level terms.
The second half started similar to the first, not much in the way of goal action, FC on top but not really breaking down the

Ossett defence. Ossett did give FC a big let off by going straight through and missing a one on one with Ashton. This seemed to spur FC into action and the chances started to come. Burns had a shot saved by the keeper, Jerome fired into the side netting, Patterson missing a sitter of his own by blasting over from 6yrds. Mind you he soon made up for that.
As a result of a poor back header from an Ossett defender, Rory found himself clean through on goal and rounding the keeper. It looked like he had taken it too far but with a "Hughes in Rotterdam" like finish fired the ball into the net to blow the roof off the MRE.
The goal seemed to finish off Ossett who lost heart. Margy decided to make a double change by bringing on new signings Thomson and Baguley. This made Chris and Jamie the first set of brothers to play together in a competitive match for FC. It also brought up the prospect of a midfield of Baguley, Carden, Baguley and Carden at some point in the future. It could be a midfield straight from a Preston classroom, four people, two surnames.
In the second minute of injury time Jerome broke free down the left to cross for Peter Thomson to side foot home a debut goal and seal the victory for FC.

The day after the Ossett game was the FC United AGM, where the members of the club met to find out about the business of the club, to ask questions of the board and general manager, to vote on resolutions suggested by the membership and to vote on new board members.
In the past the AGMs have been held on weeknights in the Methodist Hall in Central Manchester, but there has always been an issue that not every member who wishes to attend could do, due to work, travel etc so this year the AGM was held on a Sunday at the MANCAT campus in Openshaw.
The day was split into sections, with the first couple of hours dedicated to club business, finances, voting and an update on where the club was at with regards to a home of its own thanks to the board's very own Dr Brown.

There was then a break for dinner before two breakout groups for brainstorming/idea swapping. These were concerned with membership/match day promotion and fundraising. The day ended with a Q&A session with Margy and Rob Nugent.
The format of the day was spot on, it allowed for proper discussion of the business of the club and it wasn't in any way rushed. The breakout sessions were also a good idea and many useful ideas and comments were swapped in the fundraising one I attended. This must be the future of all club member meetings from now on and hopefully they will employ the comedian again to chair the meeting. He was very good, someone told me he was actually a head teacher but surely Broadway awaits him and his wit.

31st October 2007
The UniBond League President's Cup: Round 1
FC United 5 (Wright 3, C Baguley 11 21, Platt 34, Burns 53)
Bamber Bridge 0
Attendance: 585

Another night in Radcliffe, another cup competition. This time it's the President's Cup, which I believe is a cup played for by the teams in the lower divisions of the NPL. I was helping Jane look after the ball boys and girls for this game, so most of the pre game was spent making sure they all turned up ok, had drinks ready for half time and the water bottles were filled up for them to drink during the game. Mind you there nearly wasn't a game due to a power failure that affected parts of Bury, Manchester, Salford and Leigh. The lights went off at around 7.20pm but thankfully came back on 20 mins later. This allowed the ref to decide to kick the game off at 8.15.
Margy sprang a surprise with his line up for the game by naming Dale Whitehead at centre half alongside Colin Bell who was making his debut. Peter Thomson started his first game up front alongside Aaron Burns, with the Baguley brothers starting in midfield.

It only took a few minutes for Thomson to make his mark in the game as he played Jerome Wright in to drill the ball into the net for one nil. It was soon two, thanks to a cool finish from Chris Baguley from a quality cross by Wright again playing out of his skin on the left. Ten minutes later it was 3 nil as Chris Baguley curled a freekick into the top corner. It was all FC and Bamber Bridge hadn't been in the game up to this point. They did however, force a decent save from Sam when he tipped over a shot from inside the box but it was soon to be four as Nicky Platt went through and put the ball under the keeper. Just over half an hour had gone and the game was over as a contest. In fact it seemed the best way to keep an interest in the game was to count how many balls Bamber Bridge could actually launch out of the ground and play a game of "guess the age of the Brig (as I believe they are called) No 3." He looked about 46 yrs old it has to be said. Half time came with the score 4-0 and it was into the clubhouse to give the ball boys their well earned half time drink and biscuit.

The second half started in a similar way, with FC totally on top and it was no surprise when the fifth goal was scored. This time it was Aaron Burns who scored with a header from a corner from the left.

It was soon after this that Margy took pity on Bamber Bridge and made a triple substitution. The game then petered out as FC took their foot off the pedal and in truth with better finishing Bamber Bridge could well have scored a couple of goals of their own.

There has to be special mention of the Bamber Bridge keeper. Throughout the first half he had been getting the usual good natured stick from the crowd behind the goal, with the added embarrassment of four goals flying past him. In the second half, the songs continued in his direction and he took everything on the chin and played along with the songs. He really seemed to be enjoying himself, which is always good to see. I learned after the game that he was the reserve keeper and was playing his first game for a year. Bet he is hoping he can get his second in a few weeks when we visit Bamber Bridge in the league. There may also be some fireworks in store as well as the away team had a player sent off after the final whistle after some handbags from both teams.

November 2007

3rd November 2007
Bridlington Town AFC 0 FC United 3 (Burns 8, Wright 51, Patterson 54)
Attendance: 1006

With £45 train journeys and the prospect of Bridlington in November not really appealing, we decided to make the journey on the official club coach. The journey through many towns that ended in "Thorpe" and "Twistle" was pretty uneventful really, though we were lucky to make it through Huddersfield when we did, as a bad crash closed the motorway and delayed many fans.

We were in Bridlington and in the clubhouse in plenty of time to get a beer in and settle down to watch the Arsenal v MUFC game. The beer washed down some fantastic fish and chips from the chippy across the road from the ground. Looking round the clubhouse during the game, it greatly amused us to see a lady watching the match on the tele through a pair of binoculars. Now I know the game was only being shown on televisions and not on a big screen but watching through binoculars? Quite bizarre! Alas Utd couldn't give everyone the win they wanted and so we trooped off into the ground hoping FC could give us the 3 points.

Something that never fails to amuse is the PA announcer getting the player's names hopelessly wrong. A couple of years ago, at Clitheroe, Adie Orr was announced as Addie Orr, a mistake that launched the "He's unpronounceable" song. At Bridlington FC had the Bagooley brothers playing in midfield.

The game started quite scrappily with neither team taking the upper hand. A mistake from the Brid defence allowed FC to open the scoring with Burns latching onto a poor back header to go round the keeper and roll the ball into the net. The goal calmed FC down and the chances started to come with Jerome having a shot blocked and Chris Baguley forcing a save from the keeper.

Bridlington started to put their collective feet in, and a few tackles started to fly about. It was at this point that we started to notice the Bridlington No 11 who decided to get involved in every incident on the pitch, to niggle and annoy. It's always good to have a pantomime villain to boo and hiss at. Jerome on the left wing was having a storming game and was giving the rather chunky right back a roasting every time he got the ball. The No2 should have probably got a red card for putting his arm in Wright's face but the ref decided to keep the numbers even.

Bridlington had a good chance early in the second half when they broke into the FC area, went round Ashton and seemed to freeze, the striker took too long in deciding what to do and that allowed Foster to get back and block the shot on the line.

It was soon 2-0 as Wright collected a long Jamie Baguley ball on the left wing, beat a couple of players before rolling a bobbling shot into the bottom corner of the net for a cracker of a goal. That was the last action that the right back saw in the game as his manager brought him straight off. The goal of the season competition was carried on by Rory as he lobbed the keeper from outside the box to make the score 3 nil and to finish it off.

There was time though for some scamp to jump out of the crowd and replace Sam Ashton's towel with a kitchen mop. This resulted in much hilarity when he noticed and brought it to the attention of the ref, I am still confused as to what the man in black could have done really.

This incident meant that the journey home was spent making up songs relating to mops, with a favourite being to the tune of Feeling Hot, Hot, Hot:

"Ole ole
Ole ole
Sam Ashton's mop mop mop"

As you can imagine the journey flew by.

It has to be said that we will struggle to play at a friendlier club this season as Bridlington. Nothing was too much trouble for them, the staff were helpful and happy especially the small steward in front of the stand who made a point of asking the FC'ers sat there if they were enjoying their day.

A good day at a great club.

10th November 2007
Clitheroe FC 2 FC United 1 (C Baguley 56)
Attendance: 1245

It's an away game so it must be Clitheroe. Thanks to the NPL fixture computer (or abacus) and the abandoned first game, it was the third visit to Clitheroe this season and hopefully the last. After a pint of dishwater in the clubhouse we ventured out into the East Lancs cold to take up our seats in the stand. Same ones as we had sat on for the previous games, sad maybe, but we are nothing if not creatures of habit.

After an immaculate minute's silence for our fallen war heroes, the game kicked off with Clitheroe hoping for revenge for the 3-0 mauling a few weeks ago.

It didn't look too good for them as Patterson forced the keeper into a save inside the first couple of minutes.

This wasn't a portent of what was to come though as Clitheroe took charge of the game with only a clearance from Roscoe off the line keeping the score to 0-0. After a few half chances for FC it was down to Sheriff Roscoe to save the day again with a second goal line clearance.

The game continued to be scrappy and it looked like it would be all square at half time. That was until the intervention of the referee, Sam Ashton's foot and a falling attacker. A Clitheroe attack was ended with a challenge in the box by Ashton. From the other end it looked like a trip and the penalty was justified. People nearer to the action said later that Sam clearly got the ball before he caught the player and a penalty was harsh. The yellow cards given to Ashton and Nuge seemed to suggest they felt the same. The penalty was saved but sadly the rebound went straight back to Byrom who put the ball into the net to put Clitheroe one up.

As the players were going off, the home keeper, who had been winding up the FC players and fans behind the goal during the first half, decided to remind the fans behind the goal what the score was and to squirt his water at them. The ref saw this and gave him a yellow as he left the pitch. Sadly this wasn't the end of the incident……

During the half time break, I had my first stint on FCUM radio. I was asked by one of the guys who look after the operation if I fancied going on and speaking about the game etc. I must say I did enjoy doing it and ended up staying on doing my Andy Gray bit with Sam and Keith, who were commentating, for part of the second half.

A second half that started with a Patterson surge into the box which was ended with a tackle from behind in the box, this time the ref saw the touch on the ball and waved play on.

Clitheroe went two up soon after. The FC defence fell asleep from a free kick and Paul Fildes, who had played previously for Padiham against FC, headed the ball past Ashton for 2-0.

The lead lasted just a couple of minutes thanks to a fantastic freekick from Chris Baguley that curled right into the top corner.

The goal brought a stoppage in play as the ref, Aaron Burns and the Clitheroe chairman were forced to go over to the FC fans behind the goal who seemed to be tugging on the net and trying to give back to the keeper what he had dished out earlier.

Reports in the days after the event suggested that beer was thrown at the keeper after the goal. There was also alarming reports of FC "fans" spitting towards members of the board and the club secretary. Now I wasn't over there so didn't see anything happen like this directly but if these incidents occurred then the people involved need to take a hard look at themselves. I mean this specifically in the spitting allegations. The people reportedly on the end of this are people who work tirelessly for the club and they don't deserve abuse of that nature or indeed of any nature.

With regards to the possible beer throwing, the old adage "If you dish it out, you should be able to take it back" should come into play. We give the opposition players and keepers in particular stick, usually good natured and we should be able to take it back. Now I am not saying the Clitheroe keeper was right in this situation, he should dish it back in the same good nature it is handed to him. He didn't but really we should be big enough to laugh at him and not go down to his level. Easy to say after the match I know and as I have said earlier, football is an emotive game and it's easy to get carried away. Mind you the beer was so poor you can't blame anyone not wanting to drink it.

The game continued but with only really huffing and puffing from FC. Clitheroe were happy at this stage just to try to play on the break and to contain FC and it worked. Even the introduction of Thomson didn't have an effect, in fact for some reason FC just seemed totally to lose their shape and resorted to firing high balls up front, a tactic that was never going to work even with Thomson up there.

The referee criminally only added on four minutes at the end, which was not even close considering the stoppage after the goal was five minutes long and he had to constantly tell the Clitheroe players to get on with the game.

All in all a bad day all round for FC but with tough games against Bamber Bridge and Bradford PA coming, maybe a good thing to get it out of the system.

14th November 2007
FC United 5(Patterson 52, Burns 60 61 72, Baguley C 74)
Rossendale United 1
Attendance: 1691

I am trying my best to keep too many clichés out of the book but with games like this, it is very difficult, in fact it is impossible so here it is. This game truly was a game of two halves.

A busy pre match was made even madder when Keg called and asked if I could help with the radio again for the game, so I then had to rush off to the South Stand to get my headset on and let the masses of the armchair army all over the world know what was happening during the game.

After 2 minutes I could imagine many computers all over the world being turned off as Rossendale took the lead thanks to poor defending by FC. The players were guilty of trying to play

too much football out of defence and they got caught with the Rossendale captain taking advantage to slot the ball into the net. As United fans we want to see football being played as much as possible, it is what we were brought up on, but sometimes it is ok to put your foot through the ball. Maybe someone needed to remind the defence.
The half continued in the same manner, FC just didn't seem in the game at all, Rossendale were looking very comfortable with the ball, and looked like they could have scored again at any time. In fact the score only stayed 1-0 thanks to a mixture of poor finishing and great keeping from Sam in goal.
It looked as if FC had left their heads in Clitheroe as the performance was just as flat as it was there. The half time whistle couldn't come soon enough with the crowd hoping that Margy could work some magic and get the players going somehow.
It was apparent that the riot act had been read out at half time as FC looked a totally different team, they came out with confidence and were rewarded just seven minutes into the half as a freekick by Baguley was headed down by Nugent and was slotted home by Patterson to level the score.
It was at this point that the game became the Aaron Burns show, as he put FC 2-1 up with a shot from the edge of the box and then 3-1 just two minutes later with a fantastic solo goal, beating three Rossendale players before shooting into the net. He scored his third and the fourth FC goal shortly after with a header from a pin point Patterson cross. Burns had taken just twelve minutes to score his hat-trick and put the game beyond Rossendale. Burns was being watched that night by Bristol City and ex MUFC striker Andy Richie, scouting for Huddersfield and despite Burns saying in that night's programme that it wasn't a given he would leave in January, performances such as this proves that he would be more than likely be snapped up by a league club as soon as is possible, and to be honest, you cannot blame the lad.
Chris Baguley made the score look slightly flattering as he fired home No5 from the edge of the box after Patterson had gone

clear and seemed to be brought down. The ref waved play on and Baguley latched onto the loose ball to score.
The score did flatter the FC performance somewhat. The first half was possibly one of the worst performances that had been put in since the start of the club in 2005, but the improvement in the second was fantastic and showed the character of the players, character that they could hopefully take into the next game, a tough looking fixture away to Bamber Bridge.

17th November 2007
Bamber Bridge FC 3 FC United 0
Attendance: 1435

On arriving at the ground, it was clear to see that Bamber Bridge were looking forward to the game, their officials and stewards greeted us with a smile and a warm welcome. Which is totally different to the Lancashire Police force who hadn't really wanted the game to be played at Irongate at all, but thanks to persistence by Bamber Bridge, especially the hard work put in by Stu Wilkinson from their committee and certain members of the NW Lancs FC supporters branch, common sense prevailed and the game was played where it should have been. The police had spent the week warning local pubs to expect trouble and to close their doors till after the game. On driving through Bamber Bridge it was clear that happily all the pubs had the common sense to ignore the "advice" and open as usual.
I am not too sure why the Lancs force has such a downer on the club and us fans, maybe it was due to alleged "incidents" in Blackpool during the first season, I say alleged as I am yet to find any concrete evidence of any serious trouble that weekend. In fact I would say there was a damn sight more trouble in Blackpool due to the tacky hen and stag dos that frequent the town at weekends, maybe the Police should shut the pubs down there on a Friday and Saturday? It could have been down to the events in Fleetwood a few weeks previous but as mentioned elsewhere, that wasn't really just down to our fans that day. I really do feel sorry for these clubs that have over the top

policing forced on them, with the cost that incurs, through no fault of their own.
The warm welcome extended into the clubhouse, where a lovely pint of real ale was drank, and probably the best pie, peas and gravy combination so far in our journey was eaten.
As for the game there isn't really much to say. The players were outplayed and out thought. Bamber Bridge had a big strong team and FC just seemed to struggle to cope with their physical prescience.
They took the lead after 15 mins after a Sam Ashton fumble, could have scored three more before half time, scored two early goals in the second half to kill the game off, and then pretty much coasted the game from thereon in.
The FC players just didn't seem to be able to work out how to break down the Bamber Bridge team, with the only real chance in the game coming to Nicky Platt who hammered the ball against the underside of the bar.
Overall it was a poor performance from the team, one that was even worse than the game at Clitheroe and the first half against Rossendale. The one bright spot coming out of the game was the thought that the players probably couldn't play any worse which was hopefully the case with one of the title favourites Bradford PA visiting Gigg Lane for the next game.

In between these two games, the Leigh and District Supporters branch held a race night in aid of the development fund, the fund set up to help to raise cash towards the building of a ground of our own.
Around seventy people attended with the intention of having a good time, winning some money for themselves betting on the horse races on the screen and more importantly raising money for the club. The money raised on the night was approx £2000, a great total that will help towards the goal of a ground for FC United.

24th November 2007
FC United 3 (Turner 6, Baguley C 16, Patterson 90 pen)
Bradford PA 4
Attendance: 2283

Following the run of two defeats out of three games, a game against Bradford PA probably isn't the best way to try and get your season back on track. This is made equally difficult when you gift them the customary, it seems these days, first minute Gigg Lane goal. This is exactly as things worked out.
My day started with the usual opening of the ticket office which I managed to escape for an hour or so to watch MaD perform in "Course you Can Malcolm." They were down to perform the first scene of the play and promote their three night January residency at Bury Met. They went down a storm with a packed bar howling with laughter and giving them a fantastic round of applause at the end.
As mentioned a game at Gigg these days wouldn't be a game without the gifting of an opening minute goal for the away team and so it happened again with a Bradford free kick being played down the left and the ball crossed in for a free header. Not the best of starts from the new defensive partnership of Adam Turner, making his first start for FC, and Danny Jarrett a new signing from Northwich Victoria.
Thankfully it was soon one all, with another free header being scored, this time by Adam Turner. The game got even better in the sixteenth minute when a shot by Aaron Burns was palmed away by the keeper and Chris Baguley continued his good scoring run by banging home the rebound. So FC had come back from a goal down against one of the main contenders for the title and were leading two one, surely time to hold onto the lead and go into half time with the lead? Nah, its United innit so a cross from the Bradford right somehow found its way into the net to make the half time score 2 apiece.
The talk at half time was that despite the early goal conceded and the equaliser late on, the performance was much improved

from recent games and a similar forty five mins would see three well earned points coming the way of FC.
Sadly the FC of the past few games came back in the second half, as they huffed and puffed and struggled to create anything of note early on. Bradford had obviously decided to mark a little tighter as they hurried FC into mistakes every time they had the ball. FC just couldn't keep going with Bradford fancying their chances on the counter attack. It was a tactic that worked twice for them in the second half, as an innocuous challenge on a Bradford player in the box resulted in the referee pointing to the spot, which was slotted past stand in keeper Phil Priestley. They made it four a few minutes later when a quick break down the left resulted in a shot beating Priestley on the near post. So for the second time this season Bradford PA had scored four goals against FC.
The man mountain Peter Thomson was brought on to try and spark the team into life and to be fair he did get about a bit and make a nuisance of himself but it was turning into one of those performances again, plenty of huff and puff but nothing really happening for FC. It wasn't as if they were playing badly as they weren't, no one was playing particularly poorly, it was just no one was really standing out and against one of the better teams in the division, you do need someone to spark up the team.
Patterson did pull a goal back in injury time with a penalty after Si Carden had been brought down. This was another baffling penalty decision from the ref, as he turned down the appeal as quickly as he had given the Bradford one, only for his assistant to wave his flag to let him know that there had been a blatant foul in the box and yes it was a penalty to the home team. That just seemed to sum the fussy ref up, as he seemed to favour the away team in most 50/50 decisions, especially with the penalty but to put this defeat squarely in his court would be wrong.
FC United will play worse than this and win this season, a strange game where no one played badly and no one played well.

A run of three defeats in four games looks bad on paper, but there were signs in this game especially in the first half that there is light at the end of the tunnel and it's surely only a matter of time before the team win and win well.

27th November 2007
Mossley AFC 2 FC United 0
Attendance: 889

Where actually is Mossley? I mean where actually is it? I know its Tameside way, I know we came off the motorway at Ashton and for some reason went through Guide Bridge. I also know that we went up in the hills somewhere and looking through the side window of the car towards the lights of the Beetham Tower it seemed like we had driven to Chicago. I even saw a sign giving directions to places in Yorkshire. So is it in Tameside, is it Lancashire, is it Yorkshire, or is it somewhere totally on its own, its own little republic? I really couldn't tell you.
On finally arriving outside the ground it seemed that a Burberry bomb had gone off as there were loads of teenagers lurking about all covered in check. Not a good sight it has to be said. Of course they made their way inside the ground to watch the game as seems to be the norm at these away games. It seems quite sad that we still haven't got rid of the "circus coming to town" mentality that followed us around the country watching MUFC. If it meant that the home club were gathering new fans then that is good for them, but sadly I suspect that the people who our visits seem to attract won't ever go back again. It would be nice once in a while just to go to a game, just as a supporter of Atherton LR or Nantwich would do, but I suppose that can't be the case due to the background we have come from.
The game started in a similar manner to the last few, with Mossley going close inside the first minute and pretty much dominating the game. In fact Mossley went close to scoring on three occasions before FC managed to get into the game and force a chance, with Patterson going through and firing straight at the keeper. It was the first time in the game that FC had put

some football together and had got behind the Mossley defence. If only they could have done it more often, sadly it seemed that the players preferred the long ball, cutting out the midfield and playing straight into the hands of Mossley. Having said that, it was a decent game and probably could have gone either way. It could until into injury time in the first half when Adam Turner was sent off for either a foul as last man (he wasn't) or an elbow (seen only I presume by the ref.)

That decision made a tough game for FC all the more harder and it didn't take Mossley long to capitalise on the advantage as a cross from the left was dropped by Phil Priestley and despite the Mossley attackers taking an age to try and get the ball in the net, FC couldn't clear and it was one nil to the home team.

It was cruel on Priestly who up until that point had kept FC in the game with a number of decent saves.

The second half followed a similar pattern to the first with Mossley playing most of the football, but it was good to see a number of FC players digging in, especially Matty Taylor who had been moved to left back and Jerome Wright who both did everything they could to get FC back into the game. But the man advantage for Mossley was proving vital.

The game was as good as over with just over 80 minutes gone as Priestley brought down a Mossley attacker and the penalty was duly slotted into the net.

It was another strange performance from FC, again no one played particularly well and no one had a stinker, it was just not much actually happened. There was no particular spark and not much football played by the team. On the odd occasion there was football played, FC looked as if they could actually do something with the ball and looked dangerous, sadly this was just too few and far between.

There was one incident in the second half that brought controversy to the game. With FC chasing the game one of the Mossley players went down injured and the ball put out by their keeper. It became apparent that FC weren't going to throw the ball back and this upset them, which caused a pushing and shoving match between the players. It transpires that it all came about from instruction from Margy, who in response to the Mossley bench constantly appealing to the referee to send off FC players told the players not to throw the ball back to Mossley should the opportunity arise. There were also reports of a Mossley player trying to wind up FC fans in that corner of the ground by imitating an aeroplane. All in all it was an unsavoury incident that sadly didn't provide the spark needed to get FC back into the game.

December 2007

1st December 2007
FC United 2 (Patterson 11, Wright 87) Rossendale United 1
Attendance: 1744

When is a home game not a home game? When Bury manage not to get themselves thrown out of the FA Cup and are drawn at home. Due to them playing Exeter City at Gigg this game was played at Radcliffe Borough. Some like playing games there, some don't, personally I don't mind it but doing the radio commentary was hard work due to the stand being very shallow and behind the goal instead of down the side.

The first piece of good news of the day was Rob Nugent being fit and taking his place in the side alongside Adam Turner with Danny Jarrett the player making way.

The game got off to a scrappy start with neither team really getting any football played but FC could have taken an early lead when the Rossendale keeper totally missed his kick but recovered just before Burns could turn the ball into the net.

This seemed to kick FC into action and for the first time in about three games they started to play football, proper football, passing it to each other on the floor and everything. This resulted in a goal for Patterson, marking his 100th appearance for the club, when a fantastic ball through by Burns put him free and he fired into the roof of the net. The sense of relief round Stainton Park was obvious and that seemed to permeate onto the pitch as Brazilian style football was coming from the red shirts. Jamie Baguley had a shot just over and Rory should have had his second when put through again by Burns but he shot weakly at the keeper. It was clear that the goal had settled the team and the work rate was also much improved from the past couple of games as FC were getting into tackles and getting to the loose ball first. A massive improvement, an improvement that was much needed and it was a shame that FC only went in at half time with a one goal lead.

Sadly the fluent performance of the first half couldn't continue into the start of the second but to be honest that wasn't entirely the fault of the players on the pitch. By 4.15pm I would guess that there had been, at the most five minutes of football actually played as the game was stop/start due to injuries, fouls, the ball sailing out of the ground. I don't think I have ever seen such a scrappy passage of play in all the years I have been watching football. That was until an incident that was as funny as it was unfortunate.

Rory Patterson picked the ball up near the centre circle and was about to turn with it until he was dumped on the floor. I must admit I didn't see what had caused him to go down, but I certainly saw him leap from the floor and hurtle at full pelt towards the Rossendale bench. It was clear that something had been said and it wasn't pleasant. Both teams and benches all got involved in the mêlée with the result that Patterson had to be substituted and the Rossendale manager was dismissed from the side of the pitch.

As he walked off, he had to walk towards us in the "Kiss of death FM" radio position, and it was clear that he had a smirk on his face, a smirk that suggested to me he was thinking a job well done there. This was probably seen by some of the FC fans gathered near the tunnel who were welcoming him to the tunnel area in the way you would expect any football fan to do. What you don't usually expect is the manager to actually stand there and continue to argue the toss with the fans. With hindsight, it is easy to see that the Rossendale manager should have been ushered down the tunnel and out of the way, especially with the substituted Patterson on his way off to get treatment on a very swollen and very black eye. Everyone who saw Rory coming behind the goal knew what was coming next as the expected confrontation took place. I was trying to see what was happening but couldn't see due to the wall at the end of the stand blocking my view. It certainly looked like an almighty scrum so I decided to take off my headset and take a look so I could relay at least some of it to the radio listeners. By the time I had got over there Patterson had gone to the dressing room, the Rossendale manager didn't seem to be anywhere but there was a couple of fans being held back by various people. It had mostly seemed to have died down. As I have said before, football is a very emotional game and things can very easily go over the top. This was an incident that really could have been easily avoided. The guy from Rossendale should have been escorted down the tunnel and away from any potential flashpoints as I say. This isn't to criticise the club or the volunteer stewards who were doing a sterling job on the day as it was a mistake which is easily learned from.

As all this was going on, the match continued, sadly not too well from a FC point of view as the incident seemed to fire Rossendale up and they soon equalised when a cross from the right was slotted past Priestly to make it 1-1.

It looked as if the game would end in a draw as neither side really looked like scoring a goal, Burns hitting the outside of the post the nearest either team came until three minutes from time when a lob by Wright came down with snow on it right under the crossbar. Thankfully the defender stood on the line could only head the ball up onto the bar and back into the net for the winner. Cue pandemonium around the ground as FC saw out time to win the game.

It was a much needed win, one that firmly kept FC in the hunt for at least a play off place and after the turmoil of the past few games it was good to see some of the old FC back again especially in the first half.

26th December 2007
Radcliffe Borough 1 FC United 1(C Baguley 86)
Attendance: 1290

At last, a game of football to watch. With all matches since the start of December being called off thanks to frozen/waterlogged/frozen and waterlogged (delete as appropriate) pitches it was good to be back into the swing of things at Radcliffe. It also looked good for 3 points, the team had had a good rest and should be chomping at the bit just like the fans, Radcliffe bottom of the table with no wins so far and FC having the confidence of the hard fought win against Rossendale in the last game. Sadly it didn't turn out that way.

The omens looked bad before the game as Sheriff Roscoe limped out of the warm up so a shuffle in the team was needed. Liam Foster stepped up from the bench and Danny Jarrett replaced him on it.
The game started quite brightly with both teams trying to attack. Sadly there was little quality on show as both teams seemed to go to pieces when they got anywhere near the penalty area. FC had some shots over the top, one from Hanley into the side netting and Radcliffe hit the top of the bar from a cross but apart from that nothing was happening. FC had the lion's share of the possession, but the Radcliffe defence, at times nine deep, stood firm and wouldn't let FC have any clear chances.
Just as I was saying that the worst thing that could happen was a goal from Radcliffe, it happened. A corner from the left was headed in by Dawson. It was against the run of play but that just proved that if you don't make your possession count you can expect to be punished.
The second was in general, poor. Radcliffe as expected were happy to sit back and attack on the break and without the guile of the suspended Patterson, FC just couldn't break down their organised defence. Simon Carden had a good shot saved by the Radcliffe keeper but apart from that there wasn't much chance of a goal from open play. And so it proved, as a silly foul just outside the Radcliffe area resulted in an equaliser from Chris Baguley with a typical freekick curled into the top corner.
There was also time for a disallowed goal from James Holden on his debut who was adjudged to be offside when tucking in a rebound from a shot from outside of the box.
To be honest, that would have been cruel on Radcliffe who deserved a point for their organised display, a draw with both goals coming from set pieces pretty much summed the game up. Frustrating and disappointing.

29th December 2007
Curzon Ashton 0 FC United 2 (S Carden 32, Nugent 64)
Attendance: 297

Cheshire Association Football League – Division 2
FC United Reserves 3 (O'Neill 30, Allen 35, Harrop 73) v Club AZ 1
Attendance: 493

"Saturday, Saturday, Saturday is Boycott Day" to paraphrase Tiswas, but the day of the Curzon Ashton game brought a higher crowd at the reserve game at (H)Abbey Hey than at The Tameside Stadium. This of course was due to the boycott of the game that was suggested by the board of FC United in light of the decision to move the kick off to 12.45 for it to be shown live on the internet.

We were first made aware through a statement that appeared on the club's official site saying that the game was being moved and with both clubs opposing the decision, the board of FC would not be attending the fixture and they were asking the fans to do the same.

The statement made the point of saying that the club had been assured that games would not be moved without the consent of both clubs, this hadn't happened and so the request was made for supporters to vote with their feet.

The matter then turned into a "who said what and when" which to be honest has been done to death, though I do have to say that at times it did get a little unsavoury with claim and counter claim going backwards and forwards.

From my point of view, I elected a club board to work on issues such as this on my behalf and it was a no-brainer that they should be supported in their decision. Of course it is the right of the individual to decide for themselves whether they attend the game or not.

One of the reasons behind the move to form FC United was that football should not only be affordable to all, but that it should be played at 3pm on a Saturday, the traditional time for football to be played. Some games in the first season were moved to Sundays as the home clubs had to move them to accommodate the support. But they were never moved for TV purposes.

We always knew that the day would come where a request would be made for a change of KO time for a television audience, but to be honest I don't think many expected it to happen at NPL Div 1 level.

The club was on a hiding to nothing really, accept the change and get sniped at for selling out on one of the core principles of the club, reject and call for a boycott and be accused of trying to bully the clubs and league into their way of thinking. Mind you, if any of us really gave much credence to the people who snipe at the club, we probably wouldn't still be here.

For me, as I say, it wasn't much of a choice, back the board and give the game at Curzon a miss. If nothing else it would give a clear message that we are sound in our beliefs about how football and its clubs should be governed and run; not just sound bites put about by supporters of the club, but good solid principles that will be upheld wherever possible. As and when we progress up the leagues, should we do so, the club and supporters will be tested in this way on many matters and it's important not to just blindly accept what is laid out in front of us, but to see if they compromise our principles and to challenge them if possible.

As it turned out, the boycott can only be described as a success. Only a handful of FC fans, around 20, actually attended the game at Curzon with a larger crowd gathered at The Abbey Stadium in Gorton to watch the second XI play against Club AZ. The teams did their part in winning both games but the real victor on the day was the football supporter who showed that when necessary they will actually fight for what they believe in and that they will not be pushed around and treated like a commodity.

"Forever, Until Victory."

January 2008

1st January 2008
FC United 5 (Wright 13, Patterson 56 57 90 pen, Platt 86)
Mossley AFC 2
Attendance: 2017

A rarity for FC, a game at Gigg Lane. Finally, after weeks of playing at away grounds or indeed not playing at all we finally get to return to Gigg Lane with revenge on the mind after the poor 2-0 defeat at Seel Park back in November.
As there were no tickets for future game on sale in the ticket office, pre match was spent in CYCM watching the godlike genius of local singer Gideon Conn. His strange blend of folk/hip hop went down a storm so much that he sold out of CDs after his brief gig.
The game itself started brightly, both sides doing their best to attack but with Mossley playing a very obvious offside trap, something that was breached when Si Carden went clean through and round the keeper then unselfishly passed to Jerome who had the simple task of tapping the ball into the net. The lead didn't last too long as a glancing header at the near post from the big Mossley striker Hamlet crept in past Ashton to equalise. The half continued with both teams looking to play, Nugent put a free header wide, a Mossley volley flew over, Nugent then hit the bar from close range. There was even time for a missed penalty from Nicky Platt after the keeper was deemed to have fouled Aaron Burns. The Mossley players weren't happy about the decision and it seemed Platt has sympathy for them as he stroked a very tame penalty that was easily saved by the keeper. Half time came with the scores level but FC could easily have had a large lead with more luck and better finishing. It was noticeable though that the performance was a vast improvement on the last few games, this was probably due to the fact that we were playing with two wingers and trying to use them as often as possible.
Mossley started the second half as the better team, which was clearly seen by Margy as he made a bold double substitution with Burns and Carden being brought off and Patterson and

debut boy Nick Robinson brought on to replace them with Burns making his way straight down the tunnel. This had the desired effect and then some.
Within a couple of minutes Rory had put a shot just wide and it was only a matter of time before he got a goal. Inside four minutes of being on the pitch he had scored two goals. The first came when he beat the offside trap, went round the keeper and tapped the ball into the net. The second was made by a superb run and cross by Jerome Wright.
Rory also had a goal disallowed for offside which brought the comedy moment of the day as he showed his frustration by kicking the ball at the corner flag sending it spinning in the air. The referee then made him go back over and stand it back up. Just like a schoolteacher telling off a naughty pupil. Mind you with the amount of whistle blowing and finger pointing the ref was doing, he probably was a teacher.
Another of his soft decisions led to Mossley pulling a goal back when a quickly taken free kick found its way to their skipper Connor who tapped the ball into an empty net. It seemed for a short while that the game could go either way but good work by sub James Holden on the right hand side led to a cross turned in by Platt to make up for his earlier penalty miss, and the win was confirmed in injury time when Patterson was tripped in the box to win a second FC penalty of the game. Rory picked himself up and tucked the penalty home to get himself a hat trick and make the game safe. He even had time to goad the Mossley keeper by letting him know exactly how many goals he had scored during the game. Does he need to do things like that? Well possibly not, but it makes for good viewing and if it doesn't get in the way of his general play it can be forgiven.
So a good win for FC and one that gives Margy a selection dilemma upfront, with Patterson's hat trick and the excellent performance of Nick Robinson making it difficult to drop them for the next game.

The day after the Mossley game, Aaron Burns was released by the club and joined Northwich Vics. Sadly after his initial burst and goal glut it seemed that Burns had one eye on the January transfer window and didn't seem to be as willing to "get stuck in" as he did when he first joined. Whilst this is understandable, as supporters we want to see our players putting 100% in all the time. They may not have outstanding games every week but that is always forgiven if the effort is there.

With a blank weekend, some of the first team players went over to Germany to play in a six team indoor tournament. I didn't make the trip but Alison Watt did, and she recorded her trip. This first appeared in the match day programme and Alison has kindly allowed me to reproduce it here also.

On 5th January 2008, FC United made an historic appearance in the Hallenmasters 5-a-side tournament held in Riesa, Germany. Among the six teams participating were our old non-league friends from 1. FC Lokomotive Leipzig, but the standard of the tournament was clearly high as the four other participants were FC Energie Cottbus and MSV Duisburg from 1.Bundesliga (1st div) and FC Erzgebirge Aue and FC Carl Zeiss Jena from 2.Bundesliga (2nd div). We shouldn't underestimate what an honour it was to be invited and these 5-a-side tournaments are very prestigious during the winter break in the German leagues.

One of the biggest things I've missed over the last couple of years is the constant stream of Euro away trips. I'm not trying to be all superior here and anyway I've been on a couple of United trips since the takeover, but the magic has gone. I've missed being involved in the routine chaos of trying to do every European game with limited annual leave entitlement and even less money. I always loved the racing around searching for cheap flights, with the constant refrain at games of "What you doing for XXX". Leipzig was great, but it was over 18 months ago and the withdrawal symptoms were getting to me.

Then along came Riesa. The confirmation of the trip was beautifully late leading to the old adrenalin rush of chasing for planes, trains and hotels before all the best deals got taken. I'm sure budget airlines were invented for football Euro aways, particularly the ability to book one way trips, so a quick internet trawl got me on a flight out from one airport with a return to another. I dusted off my favourite international hotel booking website, which coincidentally is German and found the best hotel I could in Riesa. The Deutsche Bahn web site is always the most efficient for planning train journeys, even in the UK, so tickets were soon arranged; 1st class at that, because they were the cheapest available. All sorted and I started wandering round asking fellow FC fans "What you doing for Riesa?" only to find no one was going. Well hardly anyone I knew was up for this trip and there was a complete no show from my former gang of seasoned Euro-awayers. Ah well, I've been halfway round Europe on my own, so no problem.

Friday was a gentle trip out to Riesa via Berlin meeting up with Voxra on the way. We'd also arranged to meet later with Stuart, a Mancunian now living in Germany, who was staying in the same hotel. Riesa was very quiet on the Friday evening as the teams and most fans weren't arriving until Saturday morning, so our little band of 3 set off to find the nightlife, knowing that everyone would want somewhere to go the following night. It was useful to have Stuart speaking fluent German, although we'd been managing so far on Vox's Norwegian-German and my ability to shout in English. Stuart quizzed the locals and they told us the only nightlife open until late was a pub, which inevitably turned out to be an Irish bar. The staff and locals in Molly Malone's were friendly and keen to chat about the tournament. They also told us about their town's team, TSV Stahl Riesa, which was once a 1st division club in the old East Germany. Like Leipzig they failed to survive well after reunification and went bust in 2003. They have been reformed by fans and so far climbed from level 9 to level 7. Leipzig are level 5 now.

A late night at the pub, with more drinks back in the hotel bar meant a late start on Saturday morning, but as the tournament wasn't due to start until noon it didn't matter. Stumbling bleary eyed from my room to the lift on the way to meet the others in the bar, I wasn't quite prepared for the lift doors to open and reveal Margy and some of the team, who had just arrived to book into the hotel before the tournament. I'll never quite get over that little rush of bumping into my heroes, despite the fact that one of the brilliant things about FC United is you can hardly move without tripping over one of the team. I'm still a starstruck fan at heart.

And for a fan the next coup was even better, as all those in the hotel were crammed onto the team bus for the short trip to the Edgasarena. We even generously picked up a couple of Leipzig fans, one of whom started asking if our captain from the game we played in 2006 was in the squad. When we pointed Chaddy out to him, he got very excited and informed us all that he'd got the shorts that Chaddy had thrown into the crowd in Leipzig.

The policing was visible, but calm as it usually is in Germany and there was no segregation either outside or inside the Arena, apart from the natural separation of fans having been given tickets in different sections. Each team's supporters could wander freely to use all the same bars on the concourses. By far the biggest crowd were the Leipzig fans and our tiny band of about 40 FC fans had been given tickets in with them. Despite all the scare stories we'd heard in advance there was no trouble among the fans and no overt neo-Nazism, although I'm not pretending that there wasn't an unpleasant undercurrent of fascist views that occasionally surfaced from individuals. The Leipzig fans were delighted to have us in with them and there was a big love-in between our fans and Leipzig's, including chants from them of U-NI-TED in a very staccato fashion, which at first sounded suspiciously like the USA chants we've heard elsewhere.

If you're reading this article for a serious review of the games then I'm afraid you're in the wrong place, but I suppose I should give it a go. There were two evenly matched groups of three teams, with a 1st division, 2nd division and non-league team in each group. After all teams played the others in their groups the 1st placed team played 2nd in the other group as semi-finals, followed by a 3rd/4th place play off and then the grand final. FC were in a group with FC Energie Cottbus and FC Erzgebirge Aue and Leipzig were in with MSV Duisburg and FC Carl Zeiss Jena. Squads could contain up to 10 players with 5 on the pitch at any one time and rolling substitutions allowed.

We lost both our games heavily, 6-1 to Cottbus and 8-1 to Erzgebirge, with our goals scored by Rory Patterson and Jerome Wright. However, the scores are rather unflattering as our players were by no means disgraced and at times played some stunning close control football. What really made the difference was the experience the other teams had at playing this type of football, while we were somewhat naïve at times. Not surprisingly we finished bottom of our group and so did Leipzig, though their group was much closer. In Leipzig's game against Duisburg they were leading 3-2 with 4 seconds to go when Duisburg got the equaliser. If Leipzig had won that game all teams in group B would have been on 3 points and probably Leipzig would have made it through to the semis on goal difference. Duisburg then went on to win the tournament, beating Cottbus, the other Bundesliga team, in the final.

With both FC United and Leipzig out of the tournament, there was an opportunity for an exhibition game to be played among the two clubs in the break between the semis and the final. It was agreed that this should be a fans game, though the tournament organisers requested 3 proper squad members should be part of each fans' squad. We had Margy, Bradley Howard and Nicky Platt in our squad and the rest of the players came and sat with the fans in the stands, where they got constantly asked to sign autographs for the Leipzig fans. The Leipzig fans' team were a bit mean and chose their goalkeeper as one of their players, but this was still a much more even game than our previous thrashings. It ended all square at 2-2, with our goals coming from Nicky Platt and Margy, who was the self-styled man of the match. He'd have been man of the tournament if his spectacular lob of their goalkeeper had gone in instead of hitting the bar. At least that's what he told me to write!

We stuck around for the final and various presentations to the winning teams and individual players. When they dragged out a table of huge beer cans (think Party Sevens if you're old enough to remember them) one of our players was heard to remark laughingly, "If I'd known that's what we'd win, I'd have tried a bit harder!" That's your lot for inside tales, because the rest of what goes on tour, stays on tour. Except I'm grassing up Margy for his remark of "No one told me the rest would be taking it this seriously" – in Germany, are you kidding?

The fans were again allowed to jib a lift back on the team bus and later the supporters and the squad gathered for the evening in our Irish pub. The youngsters lasted for all of one drink, before discovering that there was a nightclub somewhere in Riesa and off they went to throw some shapes - see I've got the lingo, I could have gone clubbing with the kids; or maybe not. They missed the treat of the evening when George the kitman twice displaced the rather stereotypical German folk duo who were performing in the pub and treated us to his own brand of songs. The locals lapped it up, though I'm not sure they knew we were singing Bar Scarves Twirl instead of Brown Eyed Girl. However, we have to mention that George rather disgraced himself with his second set that consisted entirely of songs from the bitter blues of Oasis and, would you believe it, Robbie Williams. Somewhere in the small hours of the morning those that hadn't already fallen by the wayside ended up back in the hotel bar, with fans and players united by a shared hangover in waiting.

So what did we gain from this tournament? A few veteran Euro travellers got another fix of a Euro away and maybe more importantly, some young fans got their first taste of the European experience that we old time United fans take for granted. The experience for our players must have been superb playing against opponents some of whom were rumoured to be internationals on £10,000+ per week. There will have been positive team building effects of being away as a squad for a couple of days, especially as they could relax and have fun as a group of young lads out together. Plus it was an opportunity for all of us to represent FC in a good light and make friends and contacts abroad. Playing football and making friends, that's what we're here for, innit?

Squad - 1 Phil Priestley, 2 Liam Foster, 3 Jamie Baguley, 4 Chris Baguley, 5 Jerome Wright, 6 Adam Turner, 7 Nicky Platt, 8 Rory Patterson, 9 Bradley Howard.
Plus Margy the Manager and George the Kitman
David Chadwick and Stuart Rudd also travelled out as fans, being still unfit to play.

12th January 2008
FC United 2 (Patterson 40, Carden 76) Chorley 1
Attendance: 2011

This was an exciting day in the history of FC United. In the true spirit of Robbo in 1981 against Wolves, the club actually made a new signing on the pitch. Sadly there was a distinct lack of curly perms and gold jewellery as FC signed 44 year old Andy Griffiths as their new star player. Yes that is right 44 year old Andy….what?.....surely Margy hasn't lost his marbles totally? Actually Andy was the winner of the 12th man draw which was a raffle in aid of the development fund where the winner would be signed as a fully fledged member of the squad. He would have to attend all training sessions and if Margy saw fit, could actually play in the team. Whether or not Andy will take his turn alongside Rory up front remains to be seen.

The game itself saw the long awaited return of Josh Howard onto the bench as FC tried to continue their unbeaten run. It didn't get off to the greatest of starts as Chorley took the lead with a rasping shot off the bar after a slip by Micah Bleau at the back. So again FC had to come from behind at Gigg. To be honest we should be used to this by now and it spurred the lads into action as they had the majority of possession but couldn't get it together in front of goal. Chorley were doing all they could to hold on to the lead and their cause wasn't helped when one of their midfielders was given first dibs on the shower by the ref after sticking his hands in Jerome Wright's fizzog. We continued to have most of the possession but it took until the fortieth minute for them to get back on terms with a driven Patterson freekick that went straight through the wall and past the keeper who didn't seem to pick it up at all. FC seemed to turn the screw after this with the bar being hit twice in a 30 second spell with Nuge heading against it to be followed up by Chris Baguley doing the same with a shot from the edge of the box.

Chorley started the second half with Liam Foster clearing off the line a couple of times. They also hit the post with a freekick. As is the norm at home games the ref seemed hell bent on ruining a good game by blowing for every little collision and small thing. Something proven when a Bradley Howard throw in slipped out of his hands and into play. He tried to catch the ball and was then penalised for handball. Technically correct of course, but a little common sense would have seen that it wasn't actually a legal throw in, the ref could have let him take it again or at worst given a foul throw. It was all very strange.

Thankfully the every reliable Si Carden popped up with the winner, heading in a superb cross from Foster and there was even time for a Patterson penalty miss after Carden had been flattened. Probably the only correct decision the ref got right in the second half.

23rd January 2008
Manchester Premier Cup: Round 2
FC United 4 (Patterson 45 pen, B Howard 56, C Baguley 67, Rudd 88) Flixton 1
Attendance: 512

Yet another milestone in the short history of FC United. Following hot on the heels of home games at Gigg Lane, Moss Lane and Stainton Park, Valley Road in Flixton became our new temporary home. With the club looking at costs especially at home games in the cups, the decision was made to play at the game at Flixton. It was still classed as our home game, with club volunteers sporting the rather fetching steward bibs, but with a lower ground rent it was a win win all round. Flixton get the bar and catering as well as half their gate receipts, FC keep the costs down. It also helped to repair any strained relations that may have occurred between the two clubs in the past, with the heavy headed "stewards" in the first season and the lack of concession prices for children and OAPs in the second.
The match itself wasn't a bad game. It was preceded by a minute's silence for Halton McCollin, a player at Flixton who was murdered the previous week in Stretford. Flixton started well and Sam had to be at his best to stop a couple of decent chances but in all honesty as soon as Adam Carden was tripped in the box and Patterson scored the penalty right on half time, there was only really going to be one winner. Bradley Howard scored his first FC goal after a run from inside his own half. His shot took a heavy deflection and flew in, one for the dubious goals panel. Sub Chris Baguley made it three with a trademark freekick before the loudest cheer of the night for the return of Stuart Rudd who almost scored within ten seconds of coming on as sub, as a Mark Hughes style volley flew inches wide. He did get on the scoresheet with a couple of minutes to go when Patterson went through on the right and crossed into the box. Rudd drilled the ball home to mark his comeback with a goal. So the semi final beckoned for FC with a good victory against a game but ultimately outclassed Flixton side.

26th January 2008
The UniBond League President's Cup: Round 3
FC United 2 (Patterson 55, Rudd 81) Rossendale United 1
Attendance: 1554

Everyone in the main stand to keep costs down.

First half awful.

Second slightly better.

Patterson scored a lob.

Rudd tapped in the second.

Rossendale scored best goal from 25yrds.

Club broke even on game.

That's pretty much it!!

February 2008

February should have got off to a very poignant start with the 50th anniversary of the Munich Air Crash. Co-incidentally the FC game against Woodley was arranged for the 6th Feb and so there would be a great opportunity for reds to gather together and remember the great players along with the club officials, members of the press, crew and "civilians" who lost their life on that runway back in 1958. It was a great opportunity until a director from Bury stepped in and took it away from us.
On 5th Feb, Bury also had a rearranged game against Stockport a game incidentally organised after the Woodley game. This game went ahead and despite the poor weather in the Bury area it was expected that the FC game would be played as planned. I received word after the Bury game, that the FC game was off already, but there had been no official word from the club. In fact the club had issued an article on the official website that evening to let fans know that there would be a minute's silence prior to the game and no merchandise would be on sale at all.
On the day of the game, there was a message sent to let everyone know that the game had been called off. And that was it. A couple of hours later, another message appeared with a little more detail. This time the fans were made aware that the pitch had passed an inspection but the game had been called off by a Bury director. As with the Curzon affair, a tit for tat war of words erupted with Bury saying that they had informed FC that the game had been called off as early as the 22nd. Another statement was issued by FC to state that that this wasn't the case, a statement that was retracted by the club a few days later.
As you would expect, things got very emotional especially with the fans as they had been denied the chance to remember the crash at a game.
The incident was further compounded by the league who announced that they were holding an enquiry into the reasons why the game hadn't taken place.
Yet another messy incident that could probably have been avoided but hopefully lessons have been learnt on all sides. The club shouldn't try to be all things to all people at all times, and keep their counsel more. The statement denying the contact

made by Bury seemed to be rushed out due to the insistence for information by the supporters, I really feel a bland "We are dealing with the situation and will let you all know the outcome shortly" would have sufficed, it would have bought the club time to fully investigate everything. I accept that it is difficult, as many of the supporters are members and so of course are owners and so make demands for information. And here is, I feel, the second lesson to be learnt. The fans should show more patience when these matters do arise. We really should allow the employees and board members to get on with handling the situation, safe in the knowledge that when there is information to be handed out, we will be the first to know.
All in all a very undignified incident at an emotional time when really all thoughts should have been with the 23 people who died on that Bavarian runway.

16th February 2008
FC United 3 (Patterson 17 63, Robinson 90) Skelmersdale Utd 0
Attendance: 2168

After the shenanigans of the previous week or two it was good to finally get back to the football. Skem had been on a fantastic run, taking them to the top of the table, there was of course also the added spice of revenge for FC for the poor defeat earlier in the season.
Pre-game there was the minute's silence in memory of all who died in Germany on 6th Feb 1958. That was a nice touch from the club, expected I suppose, but with the "fun" since the postponed Woodley game it would be easy to forget and just get on with the game.
The game started pretty brightly, with Skem probably the better team. They nearly took the lead, but the debutant keeper Aaron Grundy, on loan from Bury FC, saved at his near post. This got FC going with Jamie Baguley almost scoring with a shot that somehow went through the keeper's legs, but was cleared off the line. It seemed only a matter of time before there was a goal,

which came thanks to Patterson, who touched in a Nicky Platt free kick.

Skelmersdale still came at FC but couldn't really force any saves out of Grundy with most shots finishing high in the MRE.

The turning point of the game came early in the second half when Skem broke through on the left and forced a flying save from Grundy, who tipped the shot round the post. If that had gone in it could easily have been a different game, Skem would have had the upper hand, but as it was it was FC who picked up the game with Liam Foster having a 30yrd shot just fly over the bar.

Foster had a hand in the second FC goal with a superb ball over the top of the defence for Rory to run onto and slot into the bottom of the net. It always good to see Rory score at the MRE if only for the celebration, will it be a laugh at a defender or the keeper, the funny walk celebration he sometimes does or a slide on the knees? This time it was a sort of primal scream complete with beating hand on chest. Still at least it wasn't a kiss of the badge.

Deep into injury time, Nick Robinson scored his first ever FC goal when he ran through the Skem defence and fired into the bottom corner of the goal. It was good to see Robinson score, esp. as his performances so far for FC have deserved a goal and also as it also slightly exonerates him for seeming to continually score against us for the likes of Salford and Woodley.

It was also a breath of fresh air not to leave a game cursing the ref. Of course there were a few strange decisions, but for once the ref seemed to actually play the game and not the occasion.

This was a convincing win for FC against the team who started the day at the top of the league. It certainly started the run in towards the end of the season and showed the intention of FC to be involved in the promotion race.

23rd February 2008
Bamber Bridge 0 FC United 0
Attendance: 1236

A return trip to Irongate and an opportunity to avenge the rather poor 3-0 defeat last time at that ground. It has to be said that going to Bamber Bridge has been one of the highlights of the season with a welcoming clubhouse and officials. They really do seem to enjoy hosting the travelling FC fans and for the second time this season looked after us very well.

Before the game we had a sit down and chat with some of the lads from Middleton. They were talking about the funeral of FC fan Ant Kelly earlier that week who had sadly passed away just after returning from Munich where he had been to the remembrance service. I didn't know Ant personally but it is always sad to hear of the passing of a fellow fan especially one who was clearly well loved by all of his peers.

The game started better than the previous one at this ground, with FC well on top. Simon Carden had a shot cleared off the line after a superb run and cross from Jerome who was giving the right back a torrid time. The best chance of the half for FC fell to Patterson who had a superb free kick tipped round the post by the Brig keeper. The home side didn't really get into the game in the first half but had a great chance when a scramble in the FC goal mouth ended with a superb reaction save from Aaron Grundy to keep the game scoreless at half time.

It seemed that the half time talk in the Bamber Bridge dressing room was to stop Jerome Wright at all costs, which meant every time he received the ball he was put on his behind. This was proven when he went in for a 50/50 ball with the Brig right back and was left in a crumpled heap thanks to the defender going past the ball and straight into his leg. This sparked the inevitable fracas involving the majority of players from both sides. Once it all calmed down, the ref produced the red card. From this point the ref and his assistants lost the game totally, blowing for every little incident but missing the most obvious ones, giving every

50/50 decision to the home side and generally having a nightmare afternoon.

There wasn't much football played for the rest of the game, FC struggled to break down the home side with Patterson coming the closest to scoring when he broke through the defence but fired into the side netting when he probably would have been better squaring the ball to Rudd who was in a better position. Bamber Bridge were understandably happy to play on the break, launching the ball over the top to their left wing and trying to score that way. This tactic almost worked when a cross into the box was tipped away by Grundy with a Brig attacker closing in to tap the ball into the net.

In the end the no score result was probably fair; both teams pretty much cancelled each other out and neither team probably deserved to take all three points. Mind you from a FC point of view it was certainly a big improvement on the last game in South Ribble.

25th February 2008
The UniBond League President's Cup: Round 4
Nantwich Town 5 FC United 1 (Wright 24)
Attendance: 873

Two of the highlights of last season were the visits to Jackson Avenue to play Nantwich Town. A decent town with plenty of good boozers, a proper ground with a traditional clubhouse/hut and good pies with games against a decent side. Ok you had the woman with the megaphone, but ignoring that, good days out. Sadly the same couldn't be said of this game. The first trip to The Weaver Stadium brought driving wind and rain, a totally soulless new stadium and a gubbing on the pitch. It didn't look good when we got there to find the blades of grass were being outnumbered by the mounds of sand that covered the pitch.

With a hectic week Margy decided to give a few players a rest with Micah Blau and Adam Turner playing at the back and with Josh getting a much needed game under his belt. It's safe to say that the game didn't get off to a great start, the pitch making it virtually impossible to play football on, though to their credit and in the true United way FC were trying to. Nothing was coming off, which isn't really surprising considering the ball wasn't even bouncing off the pitch.

Nantwich were playing with the wind and it worked for them early on with a goal from a corner curled into the box, carried with the wind and headed in.

FC hit back pretty much immediately with a cross from the left slammed into the net on the volley by Jerome Wright. FC continued to try to play football but Nantwich proved they had the knowledge of the pitch by scoring a second goal in a classic Wimbledon route one style. Long punt forward, flick on, finish into bottom corner, job done.

It was important for a good start to the second half if we were going to get back into the game. Sadly it never happened as about a minute into the half it was 3-1 thanks to a free kick curled into the top corner. It was one of those games where too many players were having an off night, or just that their minds were on the upcoming league games, who knows but it was no surprise when another corner was headed in to make the score 4-1. It might have been different if a Patterson goal had not been disallowed for offside prior to this, but you got the feeling watching the game that it wouldn't and Nantwich, who to be fair didn't look a bad team again, would just extend their lead.

The Dabbers who were congregated in the covered terrace down the side of the pitch sang that they wanted "five" and yet another headed goal from a corner gave them their wish.

So overall it wasn't a great FC performance, they never got to grips with the beach like pitch, too many players didn't play well and Nantwich just seemed to want the win more. It would have been good to continue the cup run, especially with an away trip to Goole awaiting in the semi final as well as the prospect of us winning the cup and the league having to present it to us, but in the grand scheme of things and with the hectic schedule looming, it's probably for the best that another weekend game doesn't have to be shoehorned in during the week.

27th February 2008
FC United 3 (S Carden 8, Patterson 60 90) Clitheroe 0
Attendance: 1624

It was important to get the wheels back on the road after the Nantwich game. Margy obviously thought so also by bringing back the big guns and putting out his strongest possible team. A crash on the M60 and road works on Bury New Road meant that most of the crowd were on the last minute getting into Gigg but once they arrived they certainly brought their best voices along. There was always something special about the European nights at Old Trafford and we seem to have brought that along to FC. The midweek games don't seem to be as well attended as Saturday games but the crowd always seem to make that extra effort and I am sure that gets through to the players.
FC started the game well and nearly took the lead early on when a cross from Jerome was sliced just wide by a Clitheroe defender. Rob Nugent also had a good chance but he shot into the side netting. It looked as if it would only be a matter of time before FC took the lead, but it was Clitheroe who came nearest to taking the lead with a header that produced a superb save from Aaron Grundy.
Thankfully FC weathered that and did take the lead with a goal from Si Carden who put the ball into the net after a shot from Nugent went across the face of goal. That seemed to calm FC and we went on to dominate the half. The problem tonight was that the final ball was missing. All the good work up to the area came apart around it. When the ball did reach its target the chances just wouldn't go in, Wright having a shot just wide and Chris Baguley having a shot well saved. Half time came with FC leading by the goal from Carden. The performance was pretty solid but Clitheroe looked good on the break. Thankfully FC had the solid Nugent and Grundy at the back, both playing out of their skins to preserve the lead.
The second half started very scrappily and it took some time for FC to double their lead. A free kick just outside the box was

blasted into the net by Rory. Yet another goal to add the ever growing portfolio of great Patterson goals.

The half continued to be a scrappy affair, mainly due to the linesman who seemed to be struggling with the off side rule. Time and time again he put his flag up against a player walking away from the ball or making no effort to involve himself in the play. This made the half stop start but there was still the odd chance at either end. Chris Baguley had a delicate chip tipped onto the crossbar and Nuge continued his superb performance by clearing off the line.

Patterson should have made the game safe after a shot came back off the keeper but his tame roll towards goal allowed the keeper to get off the floor and save again. He did however make the game safe in the last minute, side footing in a cross from Wright.

It was a scrappy game, mainly due to the fussy officials but FC had performed well and won the most important game of the week.

The day after the Clitheroe game, the season took yet another strange twist with the news that Nantwich had been kicked out of the President's Cup by the league and FC reinstated. The reason for this was that they had brought on a sub that plays for the U18 team and who wasn't actually registered to play in the first team. The score at the time was 4-1 and so it can be argued that he didn't actually play a great part in the game. It is easy to have sympathy with this view and with The Dabbers but the fact is that they broke the competition rules and that is the punishment. It always has been, as was proven when Bury got kicked out of the FA Cup. If common sense was allowed to involve itself in football then Nantwich would still be in the cup with maybe a fine or just a slapped wrist and we wouldn't have to travel to Bradford on a Monday night. Sadly as we see time and time again there isn't room for common sense and it is something we have to accept.

No one said that this non league lark would be easy but this season just keeps throwing up strange situation after strange situation. And don't we just love it?

March 2008

1st March 2008
FC United 2(S Carden 52, C Baguley 90) Bamber Bridge 2
Attendance: 3348

This was the second game against Bamber Bridge on two consecutive Saturdays, but most importantly the game was designated Youth United Day. The club allowed U18s to enter the game on a freemans as well as inviting many community groups, sports clubs and schools from the area down to enjoy the hospitality at Gigg Lane. There were theatre workshops and banner making classes as well as free face painting for the kids (and one or two adults as well!) as well as a penalty competition raising money for the Development Fund. The Co-Op offered free food and smoothies to all fans as well as handing out bags of fair trade goodies. On top of all this FC gave out 1000 bags to juniors entering the ground that contained a free scarf, badge, info on the club and a voucher for free entry to one more game. There was a great deal of work and graft that had gone in to make the day a success, especially with the previous two attempts failing foul of the weather, and the attendance of just short of 3400 proved that the effort and work paid off in a superb way.
With the club volunteers doing their bit off the pitch it remained to be seen if the players could keep their side of the deal and win the game, which was vital at the top of the table.
The previous week's game had been a physical encounter and this game started in the same vein with Aaron Grundy being flattened inside the first couple of minutes. The first talking point of the game came when a Brig break seemed to be ended by Grundy pulling down the attacker. After a short break whilst the striker received treatment, the referee not only refused to give the penalty, he booked the Brig player for diving. It hadn't been a great start to the game and this was made worse for FC when Rory had to go off with a shoulder injury to be replaced by Nick Robinson, who was soon involved when he was barged over in the box, the ref again saying "no penalty."

It was clear from the outset that Bamber Bridge would be happy with a point from the game and they set their stall out to niggle at the FC players. There was foul after foul, the odd foot being kept in, reactions to tackles, everything you could think of that would break up the play and make it difficult for FC to play any sort of fluent game.

Half time came with the game not surprisingly scoreless. The nearest chance was a scrambled Rudd chance cleared off the line.

Of course after a half such as we had seen, there could only be one way to start the second half, and that was with a goal from the away side. A long ball was played forward towards the Limahl look-alike playing on the left wing who looked a good two yards offside, the flag stayed down and he side footed the ball past the exposed Grundy to give the away side an undeserved lead.

Thankfully it only took a couple of minutes for us to equalise and when it came what poetic justice it was. In the game at Irongate seven days earlier, the home keeper had constantly taken his time with goal kicks, taking far too long at each one and generally winding people up. This week at Gigg, he let a Jerome cross go through his hands and legs to give Si Carden a simple tap in.

FC then upped the pace of the game searching for the lead but despite many quick breaks, the final ball just wouldn't come. There were many a time that Wright got behind the defence only for his cross to hit the first defender or for him to look up and there not be anyone in the box waiting; it was frustrating to watch and most of the crowd seemed to be resigned to another draw against Brig. That was until the final minute when Limahl broke away again and fired a shot past Grundy for 2-1 and surely the three points. The board showed there was to be two mins of injury time, so it was good fortune that Chris Baguley fired in a long range equaliser in the 94th minute.

The relief round Gigg was obvious and the gooning about in the MRE was at a level not seen since the infamous Quorn game of the previous season.

I was left quite annoyed by the tactics of Bamber Bridge. It's pretty disappointing to see a team play in such a spoiling niggling manner as they did at Gigg Lane. They are a cracking club as I have said, with a decent ground and clubhouse and friendly officials, but on the pitch, certainly in the last two games against FC, they played with the tactics of 1970s Leeds United. I sincerely hope that not losing a game doesn't become that important to us that FC descends into those tactics. If so, I feel it would take many more free entry days to get the crowds to come flocking in. Happily we have a manager who was brought up on the "United way" and I can't see that ever happening.

5th March 2008
FC United 3 (Patterson 45 73, Chadwick 55) Curzon Ashton 2
Attendance: 1879

This was the return to Gigg Lane for our big rivals of last season as well as ex players Mortimer and Giggs, who were no doubt eager to show us what we were missing this season. During the NWCL Div 1 season, we had three titanic clashes with Curzon, FC winning each closely fought game including the NWCL cup final. This run continued in the boycotted game earlier in the season, but with Curzon still going well at the top of the table it was set up for another tough game.
Curzon started like a train and had hit the post and bar within the first ten minutes of the game. It looked like FC might pay for a sluggish start but as the half went on we got back into the game. The game should have turned when the Curzon keeper was injured in a clash with Patterson, the keeper being left flat on the floor clearly in some pain. Some of our fans didn't do themselves any favours though by singing "let him die" as he was getting treatment.
The keeper played on with one leg for the rest of the half and to be honest the peppering he should have taken in the goal never really materialised. In fact it was Curzon who looked most

likely to score when they hit the post again with top scorer Norton putting a free header onto the woodwork when it looked just as easy to score.
This gave FC the kick they needed and they finally tested the keeper who whilst looking understandably dodgy, did well to keep any shots out.
Against the run of play FC took the lead with a great move including a superb dummy by Simon Carden which allowed the ball to go through to Patterson who fired into the net.
The second half started poorly as Curzon attacked straight from the kick off with Giggs putting a cross straight on Norton's head to equalise. The game was pretty open, with both teams wanting to win the game, a draw being of no use to either. Patterson fired a good shot into the side netting before he was sent through and lobbed the keeper. As the ball was dropping into the net, Chaddy ran in and nodded the ball into the empty net, he looked suspiciously offside, but given some of the performances of linesmen in the past few games there was no one complaining. It was at this point that the referee decided that he wasn't getting enough attention and his performance took on a similar one to many we had seen before. Every 50/50 seemed to be given to Curzon and there was many a baffling decision, none more so than in the build up to Curzon's equaliser when he missed a clear and blatant foul on Nuge. The ball ran through to Giggs who took advantage of a slip by Foster to score a proper goal. He celebrated by running across the front of the MRE. To be fair to him, he could have milked it further, but it made him the pantomime villain for the rest of the game with his every touch being booed by a sizeable amount of the crowd.
The game was won a few minutes later with a ball over the top for Patterson to run on to, control and fire past the stand in keeper.
The game ran its course with the ref giving as many baffling decisions as he could and Norton firing a shot just wide.
This was a vital win for FC in a game that they didn't play at their best in, but as we always say, the sign of a good team is to

play badly and win especially against one of the other top teams in the league.

The hearing into the postponed Woodley game was set for the day after the Curzon game. The league had many powers in their hands should they have deemed FC guilty of failing to fulfil the fixture. They could have issued the club with a warning, docked the club points or even kicked us out of the league if they regarded the postponement as that serious. As it was the club was found guilty of the charge but didn't have any points deducted. Instead the league decided to fine the club £500 plus £65 costs for the hearing. Which in the end, and all things considered was a decent result. I was pretty thankful that the fine wasn't too high as it wouldn't have helped the finances of the club one bit.
Hopefully that would be the end of our dealings with the league and the club could now concentrate on the run in to the end of the season.

8th March 2008
The UniBond League President's Cup: Semi Final
Goole AFC 1 FC United 3 (C Baguley 45 47, Patterson 59)
Attendance: 967

Ahh the match that never should have been….
We should have been planning a short hop, skip and jump trip over the Pennines to Bradford on this day, but instead due to the blunder made by Nantwich, we had a slightly longer trip to Goole, home of the "infamous" Gooligans. A name to strike the fear of God into any unsuspecting non league football fan.
The club coach got us over to Goole in good time to settle in a boozer for the MUFC v Portsmouth game. This is where my fears of problems at this game first occurred. For some reason, I had this nagging doubt in the back of my head that there was potential for mither at this game, I don't know why, it was just something there. Anyway during the game in the pub, a group of lads appeared cheering on Pompey and of course singing Leeds

United songs. It was a close run thing that nothing actually happened in the pub, especially when one of them decided to switch off the tele as he left the boozer.
Once inside the ground, and a superb Goole pie later, some of the lads who had been in the pub appeared in the ground and of course placed themselves right in front of the FC fans. I suppose it was only a matter of time, and of course at the sight of the expected aeroplane impression it kicked off. It only occurred for around a minute or so before the police managed to restore order and cart a few of the locals away. It was also good to see that our friend from the pub who liked to turn off televisions will need to invest in a new jumper, as I believe it is difficult to get blood out of one like that.
Now of course this raises up the issue of crowd trouble at FC games. This has thankfully been few and far between. The incidents that stand out are the ones at Salford, Newcastle Town and now at Goole. Now without trying to paint our fans as angels, each incident, without fail, had been instigated by others and there has only been response from FC fans. Of course there are two ways of looking at this, the first is to say that the cheek should be turned and any taunting should be ignored. The other says that if we have people who are willing to stand up to anyone who may want to start trouble then they may offer some protection to the people and families who come to the games and just want to watch the football. Personally I can see both sides and it isn't easy to turn a blind eye, human nature dictates that. I think that as we move up the leagues, incidents will become more common place, and as we will be involved, may well become highlighted more and blown out of proportion. Sadly there will always be a gang of locals who will want to come along and say they took on a bunch of Man United supporters, and we must always be prepared for such times. The police finally got themselves organised and formed two lines between the FC fans on one side and the local knuckle draggers on the other.
On the pitch, Margy decided to freshen things up with the upcoming schedule. Micah Bleau took his place in defence

alongside Chaddy, Matty Hampson started for the first time in midfield, Adam Carden played at right back replacing the injured Liam Foster and Stuart Rudd was given a rest.
Goole started the better of the two sides, taking advantage of the wind to have a good few shots on the FC goal. Thankfully all these flew over or wide. FC seemed to be struggling to get into the game and play against the strong wind, but just as it looked like it would be all square at half time, Chris Baguley found some room inside the Goole box to score. So we went in at the break a goal up and with the wind at our backs in the second half.
The game was pretty much over early in the second half when a 40 yard Chris Baguley shot was caught in the wind, and wrong footed the Goole keeper who helped the ball into the net. Twelve minutes later it was over as good work from Josh on the right found Rory in the box and there was only one outcome. That ended the goalscoring fun as far as FC were concerned but there was time for a Phil Power cameo. He came on, he growled, he snarled, he generally got under the noses of the Goole defenders, and hilarious it was too. Goole did pull a goal back and also had their player manager sent off for kicking out at Josh Howard.
So all in all, a pretty satisfactory day on the pitch, a maybe not so healthy one off it and FC through to another cup final.
We found out on the coach home that the final would be against our local neighbours Radcliffe Borough who beat Ossett Albion in the other semi final, and so our season would see us in a cup final, which as a United fan brought up in the 80s, is always something I appreciate and look forward to.

15th March 2008
FC United 3(Patterson 3 21, A Carden 90) Newcastle Blue Star 2
Attendance: 2048

There was something just not quite right. Newcastle were in town, the Geordie variety, not the Staffordshire one, and there

wasn't a bar code, bare torso or dodgy tattoo in sight. There were no TV shots of old blokes who were alive the last time the "Geordie Nation" (sic) won the league, there were no grey haired managers in charge who were constantly on the brink. Instead we had a team playing in blue, who brought only a small handful of fans. Ahh so there was a similarity then, the Newcastle Blue Star away following actually mirrored a Newcastle United following circa the late 80s/early 90s.
It was also strange playing a side who were already as good as down, despite it only being March and the team in mid table. This was due to the fact that they had asked the league if they could take voluntary relegation at the end of the season. The club had not attracted the crowds they had hoped for, as well the distance in travelling to away games, most of which were in the North West of England. Newcastle faced, for a vast number of away games, a two hour journey to matches, which when added up to the fact that their players work meant that playing in the NPL was proving difficult for them. It probably would have been better for them if the league had been split on an East/West basis instead of the North/South. Still as we know, the league has the best interests of its member clubs at heart.
The game started in the best possible way for FC with a superb long ball by Liam Foster being slotted into the net by Rory in only the third minute. The crowd probably expected a goal glut after this, esp. in light of the two drubbings MUFC had given the barcodes in their two games this season, but alas it didn't turn out that way, as Newcastle started to control the ball, and were unlucky not to equalise when they hit the inside of the post. In fact, the back four of FC looked at times as if they had their feet on the wrong way round as they seemed hell-bent on giving the ball away, slipping on the floor and generally helping Blue Star to find an equaliser.
Thankfully at the other end normal service was continuing as Jerome slotted the ball into an unmarked Patterson who probably couldn't believe his luck with the amount of time and space he had and he stroked the ball into the net to give us a bit of breathing space. Surely now the goals would flow? Well not

exactly, with Newcastle still playing some good football they were only prevented from pulling one back thanks to a superb Foster clearance off the line.
The second half started in a very scrappy manner with FC happy to play the direct ball forward and Newcastle playing the better football. Mind you, it was FC who looked most likely to score, with even Nuge trying an overhead from close in off a corner. But instead of the ball rocketing towards goal, it trickled into the arms of the keeper.
It was also proving to be another frustrating game for Stuart Rudd, who just couldn't seem to get into the game or get a decent pass off his team mates and his frustration was clear for all to see.
Newcastle were getting more and more into the game, and it was no surprise that they pulled a goal back. What was surprising was when a 25yard shot drilled into the corner of the FC net to equalise. Add into this another Foster goal line clearance and the game was looking much shakier for FC.
Finally Rudd managed to get a header on target which was tipped over as FC started to dominate again. His day was summed up towards the end of the game as he totally missed his kick in front of goal as he looked to score a winner.
As Kitman Gary put up the board to indicate there would be three minutes of injury time, thoughts were turning to the lost points in this game, a game that FC should have won. But in the best traditions of a team with the words "United" and "Manchester" in their name the game is never over until the ref blows his whistle, and with two minutes of injury time gone, the ball found its way to Jerome over on the left. He powered his way forward into the box and crossed the ball to the back post, where sub Adam Carden was running in. I had visions of the ball being blasted into the MRE, especially with the standard of finishing so far in the game, but Carden held his nerve, kept the ball down and slotted the ball home for the winner.
Gigg Lane erupted as the vital three points were won.
It was pleasing to see the winner scored by Adam. He has spent most of his time on the FC bench, and whilst he isn't one of the

greatest players in the squad, he always does his best when he comes on, and adds balance to the side when on the right wing, and has even filled in at right back when asked. He has done this without any moaning and complaining, and if anyone deserved to score a winning goal in front of the MRE it is him. Hopefully the goal would fill him with confidence for the rest of the season.

18th March 2008
Manchester Premier Cup: Semi Final
Radcliffe Borough 3 FC United 1(C Baguley 33)
Attendance: 837

Back to our second home, this time to play Radcliffe in the semi final of the Manchester Premier Cup. Having progressed to the final of the President's Cup, there was confidence that another final could be reached and a game against Hyde United. Sadly the game started and that dream was over.

To be fair to Radcliffe they were by far the better team, and had hit the crossbar twice before we took an undeserved lead thanks to another superb Baguley 25 yarder that curled into the top corner.

The second half started poorly with Radcliffe equalising and then stretching the lead and then again.

FC for some reason played the second half as some sort of late 80s Wimbledon side, lumping the ball forwards at most opportunities which played straight into the hands of the Borough defenders, leaving Patterson and Rudd with not much chance to get us back into the game.

An awful freezing cold and a performance to match. Not one of the best nights we have had following this team of ours.

22nd March 2008
FC United 2(J Howard 46, S Carden 74) Radcliffe Boro 2
Attendance: 2163

So the second in the week's Radcliffe double header, and fingers crossed for a better performance and result than Tuesday night. Margy made a couple of changes, Chaddy coming back into the team, Josh starting out on the right, looking a lot leaner than in previous games, and Matt Hampson starting in midfield with Si Carden. It was surprising that Chris Baguley didn't start the game after the goal he scored on Tuesday, but I suppose Margy had one eye on the busy period coming up.

It was so nearly a disastrous start as Radcliffe could have been two goals up inside the first thirty seconds, Sam Ashton digging us out on both occasions. Sam had come in for some unwarranted stick from a user of the unofficial FC message board after the midweek game so it was good to see him keep us in the game so early.

It was a generally poor start by FC, Radcliffe being by far the better side and it was no surprise that they took the lead thanks to a lob by Howson, who had latched onto a long ball over the top that was missed by Nuge.

We hoped that this would spur FC into action, but it was Radcliffe who still created the chances, with Sam again making a save after they had gone clean through again after a slip by Chaddy. This was looking all too familiar, with a performance that was continuing from Tuesday.

Whilst the players on the pitch were struggling, the crowd were doing their bit to lift them. A long rendition of "Marginson's red and white army" from both the Main Stand and MRE sounded just like the chant of "Ferguson's red and white army" that rang round Old Trafford in 1992 against Middlesbrough in the semi final of the League Cup. On that night it inspired a struggling Utd side to get to Wembley but sadly on this occasion it didn't have a similar effect, as we went in at half time a goal down and with lots of work to do.

The second half started with us going forward straight from the kick off, the ball came to Patterson on the right, who crossed for Josh to sidefoot the ball into the net. Cue bedlam in the MRE and the belief that FC would kick on and win the game. The performance was 100% better than the first half one, but of course it wouldn't be FC if they weren't gifting chances to the opposition. Si Carden headed straight at Priestley but Radcliffe were also coming close, a shot just flying past the post.
Then came the main talking point of the game when Margy decided to bring off Stuart Rudd and bring on Nick Robinson. To be fair to Margy, Rudd was having another frustrating afternoon, feeding on what little scraps that came his way and not really having a decent sight on goal. It was probably thought that by introducing Robinson, there would be more pace up front and a better chance of turning the Radcliffe defence. Anyway Rudd trudged off pretty slowly, it was clear that he wasn't happy. He passed Margy who as usual offered a handshake to the departing player, only for this hand to be shoved away. Rudd then pulled his shirt off and went straight down the tunnel, only coming back to the bench after Phil Power went after him.
Was it an act of frustration or petulance? Well probably a bit of both in all honesty. It was clear he was frustrated with his performance and the performance of the team, but it is to be remembered that it is a team game, and Margy is there to make decisions that he feels are best for the team. It seemed that all had been sorted by the time that the player and manager had reached the Swan for a post match drink, but it has to be said that incidents like that can't be good for team spirit and morale especially with the important run in to the end of the season.
Within a couple of minutes of Rudd going off, Radcliffe had taken the lead again, as Howson again went through and confidently fired past Sam.
It looked like it was going to be one of those games again, especially with Boro seemingly getting every free kick decision from the overly fussy (to put it mildly) referee. Thankfully and not for the first time, Si Carden pulled us out of the mire with

one of his trademark Scholes-esque runs into the box, picking up a cross from the right and firing it into the bottom corner. That finally spurred FC into action, all the action was on the Radcliffe goal but without really testing Phil Priestley too much, the only thing he really had to do was tip over an Adam Carden cross from the touchline over the bar.
All in all, especially with how the game went this was a point won, but the performance of the team needs to take a step or two up for the rest of the season.

24th March 2008
FC United 2(J Baguley 66, Rudd 89) Woodley Sports 1
Attendance: 1066

Awaiting FC on Easter Monday this year was the plastic pitch at Woodley Sports. The last time I had watched a game on a plastic pitch was at Deepdale back in the early nineties, when I lived in Preston. The game was PNE against Bradford City, who had Frank Stapleton as their player manager and also had Mike Duxbury playing for them. The score that night was 4-3 and I would settle for the same as long as we were the winners, though not sure if the heart could take it.
There was also consternation at the fact that the price seemed to have been inflated from £6 to £8. A few fans decided not to bother attending the game, but there was an explanation from the club that the price for Woodley home games would be £8 for the remainder of the season due to money troubles. It was a situation I reluctantly accepted. It seems a bit of a coincidence that they chose the FC game to start this initiative.
It later transpired that the travelling Bamber Bridge fans paid £7 just a week later. Bad practice from Woodley and something I am sure the FC fans wouldn't forget about in a hurry.
It was vital that FC picked up the three points from this game, but it was also important that the performance was an improvement on the last few games. Thankfully the latter was the case straight from the kick off as FC imposed themselves on the game, Adam Carden out on the right wing causing problems

for the full back time and time again and Nick Robinson, replacing Stuart Rudd upfront, proving a handful for his previous team.
All the football was coming from FC despite there not being many chances, the game taking on a familiar style of the final ball letting the side down. Shaun Roscoe and Chris Baguley both had shots saved by the keeper and Adam Carden hit the side netting but despite the pretty much total domination of FC the score was goalless at half time.
We were hoping for a continuation of the first half performance from the start of the second half, sadly Woodley didn't want to play their part and they took the lead straight from the kick off. The storm clouds gathered and the doomlords were already writing the team off, well the rather loudmouthed FC "fan" in the stand was. He only seemed to be there to moan at every little mistake, and offered no praise whatsoever to the players on the pitch.
The half continued in a similar vein to the first, with FC playing all the football, and Woodley trying to break on the counter. Thankfully Jamie Baguley chose this game to break his FC scoring duck, with a superb shot from around 20yards out that flew into the corner of the net.
Again FC pressed, substitute Rudd miskicked in front of goal, Jamie had a freekick saved by the keeper, and Jerome had a superb run and shot balloon onto the bar, bounce down somewhere near the line and out. It was impossible to say from where I was sat if it was in, though it was indicated after the game that maybe it was a goal.
Just when it looked like we would have to settle for a draw and unlike the game on Saturday, two points lost rather than one gained, Mr Rudd found his scoring boots by getting on the end of a fantastic cross from Chris Baguley and sending a flying overhead bicycle kick past the keeper and into the net. It was one of those slow motion moments, you know the ones where it all happens at normal speed but somehow everything seems to take ages, the ball taking an age to fly past the keeper, who incidentally was our old friend from Clitheroe, and into the net.

Finally when it arrived pandemonium broke out and the sheer relief was on everyone's face. A fantastic goal to win a game and secure three vital points for FC. The only downer on the day was an injury to Rory that looked like it may keep him out for a game or two. Now bring on Chorley at Gigg and let the bandwagon continue on its merry way.

26th March 2008
FC United 3 (Patterson 8 50, Rudd 90) Chorley 0
Attendance: 1645

The MRE was closed again for this game to keep the costs down, so I decided for a different slant on the game to watch from the Cemetery End. After the last gasp win at Woodley only two days previous it was hoped that FC wouldn't be dead on their feet and could pick up the vital three points.
It didn't take long for us to take hold of the game and Rory opened the scoring with a close range shot, after a quality cross from Jerome who seemed to ghost down the left wing.
This lead should have been extended by Liam Foster who played a one-two with the again impressive Adam Carden, but sadly he corpsed as he got near the goal and shot tamely at the keeper.
It was noticeable that the players were playing football at all times. The long ball of a few recent games had gone with the full backs playing the ball into the midfield where the superb Baguley brothers were spraying it about to the wings. This is the type of football we as United fans have been brought up on, and bad results can usually be excused if the team is playing decent football.
Half time came with FC still leading one nil. The two questions at half time would be just how many could we score in the second half, as only one goal wasn't deserving of such dominance, and also why does Jamie Baguley wear a short sleeved shirt and gloves? It surely can't keep you warm during a game can it?

The second half started pretty much the same as the first, with FC on top and Patterson scoring. Pretty much same as the first goal, with Wright putting in a cross from the left and Rory this time sliding in to score. That pretty much killed off the game but there was time for this season nomination for the jester's hat award. The jester's hat was awarded in the first season to the player who gave the fans the biggest laugh during the game, or did something pretty ridiculous. If the award was still going I think Mr Patterson would have been awarded one with golden bells on it. He was played in by yet another superb ball from midfield and went round the keeper with ease. It was at this point he must have thought "Shall this be easy or hard?" Of course Rory being Rory he chose the hard route and instead of shooting, he tried to dribble past the defenders who had got back. The ball then got stuck under his foot and he stumbled over it, he managed to get back on his feet and shoot. Sadly the shot was sliced and actually ended up going out for a throw in about halfway in the Chorley half.
It was left to Stuart Rudd to show Rory how to do it in the last minute as he went round the keeper and scored in the empty net. All in all a pretty convincing win and a superb footballing and team performance to boot.

29th March 2008
FC United 2(A Carden 41, J Baguley 49) Lancaster City 2
Attendance: 1859

I woke up to a text from the club that said that the pitch was playable after much rain in the week and two games on the Gigg Lane cabbage patch, but to hope for lots of wind. It didn't really say if the game was on or off, I suppose it was just a case of presuming so.
On arriving at the ground, the pitch didn't look too bad, but there was quite a bit of sand on it and it was very wet underfoot in front of the South Stand.

We were told that there would be another inspection at around 2pm by the match referee, so it was fingers crossed for no more rain and the ok on the pitch.
As I hung around Gigg waiting for 2pm, I popped my head into "Angels with Dirty Faces" which was a new pre-match initiative set up by some of the fans. It was realised a few weeks ago that there was nowhere for the children of the match day volunteers to go whilst their parents carried out their duties. It was decided to try and get use of a room in the ground where the kids could go and be looked after till kick off time.
In the room around 10 kids were all playing on Playstations, throwing darts at an electronic dart board and playing table football and board games. Yet another cracking idea, as long as it is used correctly and not as a crèche for parents to dump their children whilst they go to the pub.
The pitch was passed fit at 2pm, but just as the announcement came and the turnstiles opened, so did the heavens. The general view being was the game might well start, but it probably wouldn't finish.
There was some poor team news pre-game as it emerged that Stuart Rudd had been injured enroute to the game in a supermarket car park, news that is typical of Ruddy's season, that has been stop start with injury and suspension, this injury coming at exactly the wrong time, with him just getting himself playing well and scoring goals.
As the game got going, it was to FC's credit that they were continuing to try to play the ball around which wasn't easy on the sticky pitch. It was a shock that Lancaster took the lead when their winger broke down the left and crossed for a simple tap in to an open goal. It had been a decent opening to the game for FC and was a blow to concede a goal. It also looked like it was going to be one of those days as Nick Robinson was pushed over in the box and no penalty given, only for Patterson to be penalised outside the box for the same offence a few minutes later, and Nuge smacking a header again the crossbar.
Thankfully the luck changed just before half time with a shot from Jamie Baguley that flicked off Adam Carden, looped up

over the keeper and dropped into the net. It could have been even better a minute later when Rory went through and shot just wide.
Half time came at the wrong time for FC and also for the weather, as during the break it started to throw it down, not just a little rain but absolutely lashing down. In fact I was sure I could see an ark sailing down Gigg Lane past the main stand. The referee didn't bring the players out for the start of the second half, he decided to have a good look at the pitch once the rain had stopped, especially the soggy patch in front of the South Stand. He decided to give it ten minutes to dry off and look again. To be honest I couldn't see what difference another ten minutes would make, especially with the risk of another downpour, but fair play to him for giving it every chance to continue.
After another inspection the ref declared that the game could continue and the second half finally started just before 4.20. FC started the better team as Chris Baguley fired just over and it didn't take long for us to take the lead as a near post corner was headed in by Jamie Baguley. All through the half the rain steadily came down and was turning the pitch into a rather large paddling pool. There was water splashing up with every step and kick of the ball, but despite that, and a baffling performance by the ref it was still a decent game. Nick Robinson should have made the game safe but shot wide when clean through. Similarly, Patterson should have done better when he was sent through but his shot was saved by the keeper.
In the last minute the ball was played into the FC box, but with Nugent back and Sam racing out to smother the ball all looked ok. Sadly Sam missed his kick on the sopping pitch and lost his footing as he tried to boot clear, the ball slipping past him and into the path of the Lancaster striker who rolled the ball into the empty net.
It was a cruel moment for Ashton, especially as he had made some important blocks in the game and his handling had been superb in the difficult conditions.

There was still time for Robinson to have a header saved but it wasn't to be our day, the conditions had got the better of us and in the end we had lost two vital points.

April/May 2008

1st April 2008
Skelmersdale United 0 FC United 0
Attendance: 674

So, back to the scene of one of the worst performances and results of the season so far. Last time at Skem it was 3-1 to the home side and to be honest it could have been a few more. We just weren't at the races that night and Skem took full advantage.

It was a vital game not to lose, with the start of 5 games in 8 days, four of them in Yorkshire, games that will go a long way to determine if we win the league, finish in a play off place or if the season totally blows up in our faces.

FC started pretty well, Jamie Baguley lobbed the ball just over and Rory had a shot saved but if we were honest, the official killed us in the first half. Stuart Rudd was flattened time and time again from behind with no fouls given and the linesman seemed to be enjoying putting his flag up for offside every time we looked like getting near the Skem box. You just knew it was going to be one of those nights. Skem lived up their place at the top of the league by testing Sam, who thankfully had put Saturday's mistake behind him and kept out everything Skem could throw at him. It would have been easy for Sam to have had his head down but through the game you could hear him bawling and shouting at the players, a good show of character and one that will be needed in the run in to the end of the season.

For some reason we saw a different ref in the second half, but the same strange decisions, especially the one when Rudd was flattened just as a cross came in to him. Skem were pretty much on top in the second half, but the defence was playing well enough to cope with their attacks, with Sam again commanding his box superbly. Mind you he was beaten at one point, but yet again Liam Foster kicked the ball off the line. That was his umpteenth clearance off the line this season, I wonder how many points that has gained us so far?

Skem also had a good shout for a penalty turned down, thankfully the ref making up slightly for the one at the other end he didn't give but it was Skem who looked the likelier to score, we didn't perform when we got near the Skem box, with too many passes misplaced or crosses straight at the keeper. That was summed up when Rory tried to play the returning Dave Swarbrick in, when the better pass would have been Jerome who was on his own in the box. The ball was overplayed and went for a goal kick. Rory being Rory blamed his team mate. It was a real release of frustration, one that the fans watching were also feeling.

The game ended goalless, a result that if we were honest we probably would have taken before the game but the performance was a little flat. It also meant the three points at Ossett would be very much required.

3rd April 2008
Ossett Albion 3 FC United 1(S Carden 19)
Attendance: 456

The first game of the week in Yawkshire and not a good start in more ways than one. Due to an accident on the M62, the traffic was tailed back for miles which meant a detour through Dewsbury to Ossett, which actually got us there just as quickly as if the motorway was clear. We met up with a few others at the pre arranged rendezvous which was a curry house in the middle of Ossett town centre. A very pleasant couple of hours passed eating some fine Indian food and drinking some expensive, but very tasty bottles of lager.

The ground itself was a proper little non league set up. It was part of a full sports complex that included a cricket pitch and a superb view of the Yorkshire hills and dales and the large TV mast that was to be a constant companion over the next week. Then the match started.

FC didn't actually start the game too badly, the ball was pinging about between players and there were a few decent chances, with Stuart Rudd having the best one with a header just wide.

Things got even better when a corner was flicked on by Jamie Baguley and the ball bundled in by Si Carden to give us a well deserved lead. Then, for some reason the wheels seemed to come off and Ossett started to dominate the game. They had chance after chance, the ball flying wide, over the bar or when they got it on target, Sam was throwing himself everywhere to keep the ball out. If it wasn't for him the score at half time would have been a cricket score in favour of Ossett.
We were hoping for a start to the second half similar to the first but sadly this never materialised as for some reason we seemed to stay in the dressing rooms. Ossett were attacking from the whistle and you knew it would only be a matter of time before they pulled one back, and they did, firing in a rebound after they had smacked the bar. We hoped for a reaction, but sadly there wasn't one. Instead we huffed and puffed but couldn't get near to scoring and it wasn't a surprise when Ossett scored with a free header from a corner to go into the lead. For the majority of the half the FC goal had led a charmed life and it was only poor finishing that kept the score down.
On the occasions that we did get near to the box, the linesman's flag inevitably shot up into the air for offside. It would be no exaggeration to say that around 80% of these decisions seemed incorrect. That isn't to say that the score could be attributed to this as too many FC players seemed to be off their game and dead on their feet. Which was a worry with the games still coming thick and fast to the end of the season. I would have expected the players to tire after the fourth or fifth game of the week, not the second.
Margy decided to go with three at the back in an attempt to get the equaliser, but there was only a Robinson shot over and a Si Carden header at the keeper that even looked like getting the equaliser. It was no surprise when in injury time Ossett broke down the left and scored a third.
It couldn't really be said that the score flattered Ossett as Sam kept us in the game with some superb saves.
The week in Yorkshire didn't get off to a good start and with the players looking so jaded it didn't bode well for the coming

week, but things can only improve on the performance at Ossett and fingers crossed that the Wakefield game will bring that much needed improvement and three points.

5th April 2008
Wakefield FC 3 FC United 2 (S Carden 78, Chadwick 90)
Attendance: 1378

Part two of the Yawkshire adventure and a trip just up the road from where we were on Thursday, which begs the question why didn't we just stay there for a couple of nights? Well we didn't and it was back over the M62 yet again this time early to avoid any possible repeat of the traffic problems from Thursday.
We eventually found the ground, despite following the home side's directions which were poor to say the least.
The ground itself was a decent little set up, with a nice big clubhouse and Astroturf pitch for hockey etc. Maybe another possible blueprint for our future ground, though I think we can safely avoid the plastic covered standing section.
Talking to a couple of home fans it became clear that they were a little unhappy with their club who had decided to charge £1 to sit in the stand. They usually don't have to pay for this privilege and so were understandably upset. They also said that the programmes were usually free, but they were £1.50 for this game, also out of order by the home club.
As for the game, Margy decided to freshen things up, giving both Rory and Stuart a place on the bench, Robinson and Power playing up front. Kyle Harrop stepped up from the ressies at right back and James Holden partnered Si Carden in midfield.
FC started the game well, there was lots of nice football played between the players and chances were being created. Jerome had a shot blocked and Nuge headed just over, it looked just a matter of time before we took the lead. Sadly, as the games seem to be going lately, we actually went a goal behind. A long cross from the left eluded everyone including Sam, and after a bit of a scramble at the far post the ball was bundled in. Happily this didn't seem to deflate the players too much as they were still

making chances. Jamie Baguley was unlucky to see a shot go just over the top. But half time came with the score at one nil to the home side and Margy with a little bit of work to do.
Sadly the second half started flatly, for both teams, with the game being a little scrappy, Swarbrick was sent through on goal but hesitated and the keeper saved. This seemed to wake the teams up, with Wakefield having a shot cleared off the line and FC shooting and heading wide. We were still having the lion's share of the ball and it looked like we would be on level terms soon when Wakefield broke from defence, left Rob Nugent treading water, the games clearly starting to catch up with him, and extended their lead. It was a cruel blow for FC but thankfully it only took a few minutes for us to get back into the game with Si Carden again being in the right place at the right time to put in a rebound after Power had hit the bar.
Despite many of the players looking dead on their feet, we still poured forwards trying desperately to get the equaliser, Nuge and Rudd both heading wide, and Stuart then having a shot into the side netting.
With FC pushing forward for the equaliser it was probably inevitable that we would be caught on the break and it happened, Wakefield breaking through again for 3-1.
We never gave up and a superb finish by Chaddy almost straight away gave us a little hope, but sadly it was too little, too late and it was three more points lost.
There was one big plus point in the game with the superb performance of Kyle Harrop at right back who certainly looked the part, flying into tackles and distributing the ball well, but with the players looking so jaded, it looked a big job for Margy and his team to build the players up for the big game looming at Bradford.

7th April 2008
Bradford Park Avenue 0 FC United 0
Attendance: 1264

And so on we continue, this time to the Horsfall Stadium to play fellow promotion contenders Bradford PA. This was a game that we couldn't afford to lose, though with the previous two results, three points were really required. Considering we were looking for our first win against PA in four attempts it looked a tall order.

Pre game it was time for a curry at the Karachi, never mind the travelling that we had been doing over the last week or so, the waistline was taking a bigger hammering than usual.

On arriving at the ground we were boosted by the news that Nicky Platt was fit and back in the side, something that could only help the side, a tackler in the middle of the pitch is something that has been missed in the past few weeks. The Baguleys have been playing well in the midfield but there have been times when we just needed someone to put a tackle in and break things up.

FC started well and could have taken the lead but Jamie Baguley's shot was headed away from the line as it was going in. On the pitch the game was pretty even with some good football being played by both sides, FC probably controlling possession but Bradford looking very dangerous on the break. The football seemed to have an effect in the stand as the FC fans gathered there were in superb voice. The noise coming from the stand was awesome with yet another rendition of "Marginson's Red and White army" which went on for ages. It was clear that this was spurring the players on with Rory shooting wild and wide and Rob Nugent heading wide when he should have done slightly better. It also seemed to be having an effect on the Bradford players with them having a couple of shots wide.

It was also clear that they had marked out Rory for special treatment, which is what he had to have after one tackle from behind which cleared him out. It's a shame when teams, especially at this level, resort to these tactics, especially a team such as Bradford who are one of the best teams in the league, they don't really need to do it. The fans who pay their money deserve to see the better players actually play. It really is something that really annoys and winds me up.

Half time came with no goals but plenty of entertainment. We had enjoyed most of the ball and had a few half chances, the ball was just not dropping where we wanted it to, but Bradford looked very dangerous on the break.

The second half started in a strange way with FC starting with just nine players, Jerome and Rory obviously caught short as they were coming out on the pitch. The first chance actually fell to Rory who as in the first half shot wildly and the ball flew wide.

Bradford were seeing more of the ball in this half but it had to be said that the FC defence were playing out of their skins and were outstanding. It is rare when you get four players playing so well together at the same time, but this game was one of them. You couldn't pick one of them out for special praise, they were all magnificent.

At the other end, the half chances were still coming, Si Carden had a shot that was sadly was straight at the keeper, and Rory still being kicked every time he was on the ball. Having said all that it was hearts in the mouth time when Bradford finally got away down the left and crossed, Sam proving his worth to the team by making a superb one handed block. Then again, he did lose his head a short time later when he headed the ball clear then decided to go on a run with it, he lost possession but thankfully the shot was sliced wide.

The atmosphere in the second half was probably even better than the first; it was a non stop wall of noise, an atmosphere rarely seen since the first season. The strains of "Marginson's……." went on and on as well as the usual Old Trafford classics and it was good to see the players put in a performance on the field to match the one off it.

The game ended with a touchline fracas, Bradley Howard getting involved with the Bradford winger. There was a few raised hands and a bit of push and shove but the referee kept his

cards in his pocket when it wouldn't have been a surprise if a couple of reds had appeared.
So the game ended goal-less, which wasn't a bad result taking in the recent scores and performances. With a little more luck in the opponent's box, FC would have been taking three points back over the Pennines with them. Three points that must surely be secured at Harrogate in the last game of the week in the land of sheep, puddings and Dickie Bird.

9th April 2008
Harrogate Railway AFC 1 FC United 3(Rudd 49 54, C Baguley 83)
Attendance: 365

When your backs are against the wall and you need a result you look for any little omen that the result will go your way. Entering a chippy near the ground and being told "Our chips are cold" wasn't really the best start to the night. Thankfully the night did improve.
The set up at Harrogate is pretty good, a traditional clubhouse albeit a short walk away, with a pool table and dart board and of course the pitch with the obligatory non league slope. In fact the slope at Harrogate was probably steeper than the ones at Clitheroe and Ossett put together. From behind the goal it actually looked like it was heading down towards a cliff face, such was the sheerness of it.
Margy decided to freshen it up a little with Si Carden and the water treading Rob Nugent given much needed rests. Chris Baguley and Shaun Roscoe came in to replace them but sadly the game didn't start in the same vein as the one on Monday. It was defiantly a case of "After the Lord Mayors show" as FC looked a yard off the pace and as if the run of games had finally caught up with the players. The passes were going astray and there was a lack of spark in the players. Thankfully though Sam did have a spring in his step, with a superb save to keep out a Harrogate volley. The tiredness of the players was summed up

with Rory firing poorly wide after a Rudd flick on, a sharp and alert Patterson would have at least made the keeper make a save. It came as no surprise when Harrogate finally took the lead, though it needed a penalty after a clumsy challenge in the box. There was plenty work to do in the second half and FC looked keen to do it, coming out a good five minutes or so early for the second period. This paid off straight away as Stu Rudd surged into the box early on and slammed the ball into the bottom corner to equalise. Things improved even more five minutes later as he was played through and calmly lobbed the Harrogate keeper to put us into the lead.

The goals certainly geed up the players and they started to produce some great football. Rory was unlucky hitting the bar with a rasping shot and not even a cat on the pitch could stop the momentum. It has to be said that you don't see enough animals on football pitches these days. There used to be nothing finer than a dog that had managed to get into Old Trafford and run onto the pitch holding up play whilst the players chased it round trying to catch it. There were still some scares at the back and Harrogate could have easily equalised with a shot that hit the stanchion at the back of the goal, but thankfully Chris Baguley calmed the nerves with the third goal, firing in after a scramble in the Harrogate box.

This game saw the lowest crowd for a competitive FC game which wasn't too surprising considering the recent run of games. It was also the game where a new song was born. To the tune of "Viva Ronaldo" which had been "rocking" MUFC games this season came:

Power and Margy
Power and Margy
Standing on the wing, hear United sing
Power and Margy

Another one to add to the ever growing song list at FC and at least it isn't to the tune of The Frog Chorus.

So finally we had collected three points in Yorkshire and in the end it wasn't that bad a week. Ok we lost two games, but with two draws against fellow title rivals and the three points against

Harrogate, it kept us firmly in the hunt for a play off place, and still with an outside chance of winning the league.

12th April 2008
FC United 5(Rudd 14, Nugent 20 70, Patterson 27 52)
Lancaster City 2
Attendance: 2704

The last Saturday home league game of the season and it has to be said probably the busiest one, certainly since the Bamber Bridge Youth United day.
As well as tickets being on sale for the forthcoming game at Garforth, there were two football teams down to act as ball boys (to put that into context, there were 26 kids down when usually there are 10-14) as well as Mike Duff launching and signing his new book in CYCM alongside a troupe of belly dancers (no, me neither....)
The game was billed as "Reds Reunited" day, a chance for people who had become lapsed FC match goers to come along to watch the team and see old friends. For various reasons, quite a few people who attended the games in the first two seasons don't come along now, so the game was billed as a chance to show that things haven't really changed since those early days. The crowd of around 2700 would suggest that a few people took up the invitation, fingers crossed that they will get back into the habit again in time.
On the pitch the game started with the customary early away goal. I am told that it was offside, I didn't see it as I was still at the ticket office, but thankfully I just arrived in the ground to see Stuart Rudd lob us back onto level terms. I must admit, I wasn't sure exactly who it was who had scored at first due to the majority of the players having their heads shaved. Only Nuge and Si Carden seemed to have managed to avoid the clippers in the week leading up to the game.
We were only on level terms for a matter of minutes before Lancaster went down the left and scored with a shot into the corner of the net. It was looking like one of those days,

especially when Si Carden went clean through and fired his shot at the keeper. But cometh the hour, cometh the Nuge, who equalised by bundling a corner into the net. It was good to see Rob score, he seemed to struggle more than most during the recent run of games as seen when he looked as if he was running in treacle during the game at Wakefield.

To be honest, it was a good game, Lancaster were clearly buoyed by their draw at Gigg a fortnight before and fancied their chances of getting something from the game. Shame no one told their keeper.

A fairly tame shot from Rory from around 20 yards seemed to be easy for the keeper, it was straight at him at chest height. No one could have expected him to then spoon the ball up and over his own head into the net to put FC in the lead. It was the break we pretty much needed, and it could have been even worse for him just before half time as he made a save and ended up stepping backwards towards his own goal line. The ball was very close to being over the line, from my vantage point it looked like it was over, but the linesman waved away the appeals.

Soon after halftime, the game was settled by Rory with a run and low shot that beat the keeper. That goal seemed to knock the wind out of Lancaster and at that stage there was only going to be one team who would score again. FC did get another thanks to the unshaven ginger head of Nugent and the game was safe. There was time for Adam Carden to hit the post with a shot, and considering that with his shaven head he had seemed to lose half his body weight that was some going. Lancaster also hit the post, but in all honesty it would only have been a consolation. The win was certainly done the hard way but the team showed superb fighting ability to come from behind twice and with only four league games to go a play off place must be pretty much assured for the team.

Mind you, with bogey team Radcliffe and the imitation Uruguay team of Garforth still to come, anything is possible between now and the end of the season.

15th April 2008
Radcliffe Borough 0 FC United 2(Robinson 14, Baguley 18)
Attendance: 743

Sigh, another trip to Stainton Park and another game against our neighbours Radcliffe. This was the fourth game of the season against Boro' and we had yet to actually win one. Two poor draws in the league and an awful performance in the Manchester Cup was all we had to show. It was vital to get the three points going, to keep the momentum of the past couple of games up and to cement that play off place.

Margy seemed to have one eye on the upcoming President's Cup final against erm, oh yeah Radcliffe, as he gave a couple of players their debuts, as well as playing some of the fringe players.

It was good to finally put a name to the bloke we had seen warming up with the players for the past few weeks, every time I asked who he was I was told either "I dunno" or "It's Sam Ashton's mate" so welcome to the first team Rob Howarth. He was playing in central midfield with Jamie Rother, a young lad from the reserve team, who had impressed in a pre season reserve friendly at Atherton Collieries.

The game started pretty scrappily with neither team really playing any football, Sam had to make an early save but it was only when FC took the lead thanks to Nick Robinson that the game settled down and FC took control. It was a pretty good goal from Robbo, thankfully it was a shot taken from outside the box, as any nearer it would probably have been missed. Well he hasn't got the nickname "Jigsaw" for nothing you know.

It didn't take long for the second to be scored, this time a superbly taken goal by Chris Baguley who collected the ball with his back to goal, turned and rifled a shot into the net.

We were playing the better football with the two new lads in midfield standing out, but Radcliffe were having a few chances of their own. Thankfully their strikers had left their shooting boots at home and when they did manage to get their shots on target, Sam was on fine form keeping the ball out.

Jamie Rother almost marked his debut with a superb goal, but his swerving shot was well tipped over by Phil Priestley in the Boro goal.
Half time saw a couple of changes by Margy as Rudd and Patterson came on for Robinson and Baguley. Straight away Stuart was sent through for a one on one with Priestley, but the Boro keeper kept the ball out. At the other end Radcliffe were having a few chances of their own, but again Sam was performing miracles to keep the ball out especially one save from point blank range and a tip over from a volley that had goal written all over it.
In truth the second half was a bit of a damp squib as far as FC were concerned, the two first half goals had made the game safe, you got the feeling that if Radcliffe had managed one of their own, there were still some gears that we could go through and score another goal of our own. It was also a little understandable with a cup final only two days away.
In the end a vital three points were secured, which took FC up to third in the table and surely now another couple of points would secure a play off place.

17th April 2008
The UniBond League President's Cup Final
FC United 2(C Baguley 82, Rudd 90) Radcliffe Borough 0
Attendance: 1753

The omens were good going into this final. We had a 100% record at The Tameside Stadium, beating Curzon in all three games we had played there, including last season's NWCL cup final. We had also broken the Radcliffe hoodoo, so all looked promising for another pot in the cupboard.
The day had started early in the day in a nice little pub in Ashton and continued outside the ground, where the players were drunkenly serenaded by us as they entered the ground, Nick Robinson particularly liking his ditty which reminded him that he was actually cup tied.

FC nearly took the lead inside the first minute, but Nuge's header was cleared off the line. It was good to see that we had started the final in such a positive way, clearly we had carried the momentum from the win at Radcliffe into the game. Sadly though there was no early goal as the final ball was missing. This didn't deter the FC'ers in the covered terrace who had the place rocking with plenty of songs, some scarcely heard these days. That was probably something to do with quite a few lapsed fans who had come along to watch the game, again as with the Reds Reunited day they will hopefully return to the fold.

On the pitch the game was fairly even. Sam kept Radcliffe out with a save with his feet and Priestley in the Boro net plucked a couple of dangerous looking crosses out of the sky before they arrived at their intended targets.

FC had just shaded the first half, and you felt with just a little push up the gears, the game was there to be won.

Sadly the football of the first half didn't materialise at the start of the second as it was a scrappy start. Rory was sent through but Priestley took the ball off his toes.

In all honesty the second half was poor as a game of football. Both teams tried to get the ball down and play, but a mixture of cup final nerves and the poor Curzon pitch saw made it difficult to play football and it showed in the performance of both sides. It is easy to see why Curzon seem to get handed most of the finals off the pitch, the ground is pretty decent, good facilities and a large terrace where a decent atmosphere can be produced, but the pitch is atrocious. It was awful for last year's final, with it actually resembling the Gobi desert more than a football pitch, and whilst not quite as bad this season, it was still very rutted in the middle and in front of the main stand which made for difficult playing conditions. Add in a strong biting wind and it was no surprise that neither team could get any football going and extra time and penalties were looming nearer and nearer on the horizon.

Then Margy stepped in. He took off Si Carden who wasn't having his greatest game in a red shirt and replaced him with

Chris Baguley. It took Chris just six minutes to open the scoring by heading in a superb Stuart Rudd cross. The stadium erupted as the fans celebrated the breakthrough. Surely the goal would settle FC into finishing off the game and winning the cup? Sadly Radcliffe had other ideas and the scores were only kept level thanks to Liam Foster's thirteenth goal-line clearance of the season. Liam has made the right back spot his own this season after showing plenty of promise last season covering for Matty Taylor. His performances, especially since Christmas have been nothing short of superb and he has earned the right to claim the right back position as his own this season.

That galvanised FC to kick on and Rudd made the game safe with a pile driver into the roof of the net after a superb ball through by Adam Carden, another unsung hero of the past few games.

Despite pleas for people to stay off the pitch, there were a few kids who ran on at the final whistle, to be joined by more after the cup had been presented to the team. Whilst not ideal, it is good to see fans and players celebrating a cup win together on the pitch and hopefully it is a sight we will see repeated in the coming years, players and supporters celebrating side by side.

19th April 2008
Newcastle Blue Star 0 FC United 4(Patterson 39, Wright 49, Chadwick 73, Robinson 86)
Attendance: 647

An early start for this game as the coach left town at 9am. This was the furthest we had travelled for a competitive match and I have to say that in those dark days of 2005 I hadn't envisaged travelling up to Newcastle to watch a game of football for a good few years but here we are just three years later going up to the land of Viz, Spuggy, Byker Grove and wearing T shirts in snow blizzards, watching our red shirted team take on the might of Geordieland.

Blue Star play at the ground of the Newcastle Falcons RU club and a damn fine ground it is too. It is certainly something to look at when designing our own home, with a couple of good terraced ends and a superb seated stand all down one side of the pitch. The bar in the main stand was also superb, plenty of screens round the wall to watch the televised sport, a pool table and well priced food and drink. Everything we could hope for in a ground.

Before the game we got talking to a local fan who had come along to see what the fuss was all about. He had a season ticket at St James's Park but was more than clued up and interested in what we had done at FC. He left the clubhouse knowing pretty much all there was to know about us and with a copy of Under the Boardwalk under his arm. Again it is always good to see someone outside the FC family "get it".

Newcastle started the game very brightly and nearly took an early lead with a overhead kick that clipped the top of the bar but it was FC that took the initiative with Chris Baguley having a freekick saved and Jerome giving the Newcastle right back an absolute torrid time. FC were certainly commanding the ball but were struggling to turn the possession into chances and it was Blue Star who came closer to scoring when they went clean through, but as he had done many times in the past few games, Sam pulled off a superb save.

This was the kick we needed and the chances started to arrive, Ruddy went through and saw his shot saved and Rory also had a good turn and shot tipped wide.

Thankfully we took the lead off the resulting corner as Rory flicked a header goalwards that hit the join between crossbar and post and bounced out. It was clearly a goal, thankfully the referee agreed and pointed to the centre circle.

The game was pretty much over four minutes into the second half as Stuart Rudd flew down the right wing and crossed for Jerome to sidefoot the ball in at the far post. After this Newcastle looked a tired and beaten team, only ex Middlesbrough defender Dean Gordon looking like he might score with a free kick that shaved the post.

The ease of the game on the pitch was reflected in the stand as members of the Yorkshire supporters branch, ably assisted by a

couple of board members, entertained everyone by sitting in a line and pretending to be rowing a boat. This promoted a chorus of "Oops upside your head" from the masses behind the goal and the rowers giving us a lovely rendition of the dance that usually accompanies that song.
Back on the pitch Chaddy headed a corner in for 3-0 and Adam Carden fired over before Jigsaw Robinson belied his nickname by scoring the fourth goal from close range. Maybe he doesn't go to pieces in the box after all. We also had time from another cameo from Rory doing his party piece of standing on the ball. So it was a good performance from FC and great result, especially with results elsewhere going for us. Bradford PA lost and Curzon only drew, meaning that with good results elsewhere and six points from FC, the title could be clinched a week later at Garforth, and who would have said that just a couple of weeks ago?

Two days after the Newcastle game, I was sat listening on the internet to commentary of Bradford PA versus Ossett Albion via the mobile of George the Kitman, ably assisted by Bradley Howard, Liam Foster and Chris Baguley. Now if you had said three years ago that I would have been doing that, I would have thought you had dropped from another planet, but this punk football (and in this case punk radio) has started to make me do some strange things. And long may that continue.

23rd April 2008
FC United 1(Wright 90) Woodley Sports FC 1
Attendance: 1558

And so to the last home league game of the season. With Bradford winning two days previously, it was vital that FC won this game, and with a nine goal difference in the favour of Bradford an attacking performance was also required.
Sadly neither of these transpired.
The game started on a sad note, with a minute's silence in memory of FC supporter Fred Garner who tragically died in the

North East after the game against Newcastle. Due to this, understandably, there was a strange muted atmosphere at the start of the game. This seemed to get to the players on the pitch as Woodley started the game brightly and had a few chances to score. Thankfully they seemed to have left their shooting boots at home and Sam wasn't really put under much pressure and had no real saves to make.
We did start to get a grip on the game and a few chances came, Rory blasting a shot just wide and Jerome having a goalbound shot blocked but it wasn't a great performance by FC. Maybe it was the nerves getting through to the players knowing that a win was vital if we were to win our third title in three years, or the busy period of the past few weeks had finally caught up with them but most of the players were totally off their game.
Half time came with the hope that a few words from Margy would gee the lads up and get us the three points.
The second half got off to a poor start as Chaddy didn't make it out, being forced out of the game with a hamstring injury. Nick Robinson came on and played as a makeshift centre half against his former club.
FC got off to a much better start and started to trouble the Woodley keeper. He spilled a Nicky Platt shot, but sadly the FC players were second to react and the ball was cleared. Jerome had a cross cum shot turned wide by Rudd and Chris Baguley had a shot straight at the keeper.
Of course, as soon as FC started to get on top, they went a goal behind. The ball was pumped forwards from the touchline by the Woodley left back, looped over Sam and dropped into the back of the net. I was stood behind the goal in the Cemmy end and it seemed that Sam just lost where his post was and thought the ball was soaring wide, as did I. Only the Woodley player will know if he meant to shoot, I would wager that it was an attempt to cross the ball and it was a fluke. But when it doesn't go your way, it doesn't go your way.
The goal seemed to deflate the FC players and to be honest it was Woodley who were the better team, and they very nearly

made it two but thankfully they blew the one on one and slid the ball wide.
Slowly but surely, we got back into the game but the ball just wouldn't drop for us in or around the box. It bounced around, but wouldn't drop at the feet of a player who was in a position to score. To be fair to Woodley, they were defending with their lives, especially ex FC player Danny Jarrett who unsurprisingly was having the game of his life.
Rory did manage to break the defensive shackles and went clean through, sadly the Woodley keeper was equal to him and saved his shot with his feet.
Just as the scoreboard clicked over to 90 minutes and it looked as if FC would have to settle for no points a long ball found Jerome over on the right. He collected it superbly and steamed into the box before blasting a powerful shot into the top corner of the net for the equaliser.
Gigg Lane erupted and with three minutes of injury time to play, there was still time to save the title challenge. Nick Robinson was pushed up front and he almost gained three points for FC from a Patterson cross. Robbo slid in, but just couldn't quite make contact with the ball and it went agonisingly out for a goal kick. There was also time for a Patterson shot, but this was straight at the keeper and that was that. The ref blew his whistle and FC's title challenge had ended. With Curzon losing at Newcastle, Bradford were crowned champions and FC moved up into second place, meaning that if they matched or bettered the Curzon result in the last league game of the season at Garforth, FC would be guaranteed at least one home game in the end of season playoffs, two should we get to the final.

26th April 2008
Garforth Town 1 FC United 2(J Baguley 54, Platt 76 pen)
Attendance: 1215

And so to the last league game of the season. The play off place was secured, it was just a case of if we would finish second or

third in the league. All that was needed was a win and the runners up spot would be secured.
In the weeks leading up to the game there were all sorts of rumours and stories flying around that a mob of Leeds Service Crew were going to show up at the game and be after smacking all and sundry. Usually these can be taken with a pinch of salt, but it could of course never be ruled out. Personally I always thought that there would be minimal trouble at the ground, if indeed any, with any hassle being in the town centre. As it turned out reports pre-game were that there was no one around in Garforth, the pubs perhaps wisely weren't showing the Chelsea V MUFC game, but there were no roaming Yorkies looking to terrorise any Fc'ers out and about.
In fact there was no sign of any Leeds lads at all until just before kick off when a mob were frogmarched in by the police and after a long discussion with the police outside the ground were allowed in.
It took about 15-20 minutes for a Munich chant to start up, which was the catalyst for a few reds to arrive on the scene and dish out their version of justice. There were a couple of standout moments in all this that actually made me laugh out loud. The first being the young lads who had started the singing scarpering as fast as their little legs could carry them, through the gate and out of the ground, and secondly the Garforth substitute somehow going head first over the fence round the pitch.
Calm was soon restored, in all truthfulness it was something and nothing. As the scuffle was finishing there seemed to be an incident behind the stand towards the bar area, but I can't comment on that as I couldn't see what was going on from my seat in the stand.
On the pitch the game was being played out as an end of season game. Earlier in the season I was critical of Garforth for their very physical approach to the game at Gigg Lane where they beat FC by basically kicking them off the pitch, but to be honest they actually played football as it was meant to be played in this game. They certainly started the better team and made Sam save from a free kick from outside the area. As the half went on, FC

started to get into the game, Stuart Rudd had a shot deflected over and Nicky Platt was very unlucky when he volleyed against the post.
The second half started as the first finished with Platty smacking a shot against the post and Garforth forcing Sam to save at his near post.
The nerves were slightly settled after a good run by Adam Carden on the right found Jamie Baguley whose shot deflected past the keeper to send the FC fans all around the pitch into raptures.
Of course, as mentioned on many occasions, it wouldn't be United if we didn't let our opponents into the game and ten minutes later Garforth were level with a free header from a corner. And so it was back level and without knowing how Curzon were doing it meant we had it all to do again in order to claim the runners up spot.
The chances came thick and fast for FC, Phil Power going through and having a shot saved and Si Carden smacking the bar with a shot. It looked for all the world it was going to be one of those days but as often happens in football, just when you think your luck is out, it turns your way. For some reason one of the Garforth defenders decided to flick a FC corner off the line with his hand. It looked like he could easily have got his head to it, but for some reason decided to throw his hand at the ball. Maybe he was bored, maybe he had somewhere else to be at the end of the game and the red card would come in handy? No one will know but he got his early bath and Nicky Platt slotted home the penalty to put FC back in the lead.
This killed Garforth off and the game petered out with FC going close through Nuge and Power.
It was a relief to hear the final whistle, especially as it became known that Curzon had been pasted 4-1 at Skelmersdale so second place was confirmed and with Bamber Bridge drawing with Clitheroe and Ossett being beaten by Radcliffe it would be Brig heading to Gigg Lane for the play off semi-final.
It has to be said after some of the tribulations on and off the pitch, the spats with the league and Bury, the many postponed

games and the blips in October and April, everyone at the club deserves the thanks of all the fans for a runners up spot, a chance for promotion and a cup win when at times none of that looked possible.

30th April 2008
NLP First Division North, Play Off Semi-Final
FC United 3(A Carden 22, Patterson 38, Wright 69) Bamber Bridge 2
Attendance: 1820

Now straight away I have to make my position clear on play offs. I don't like them. I don't agree with them, I don't think they should happen. The number of teams relegated from a division should be matched by the number of teams coming up, and this should be based on position finishing in the league. A team finishing second in the league should go up, not have to play off with a team finishing fifth. It's as simple as that. Look at rugby league, you have a league season which is just jockeying for position and then a glorified cup competition to decide who the champions are. At least in football the team finishing top of the league wins the damn thing I suppose. Having said that, with FC in the playoffs, I was giddy as a kid in a toffee shop before the game so I suppose part of me actually does have some sort of soft spot for the play off system.
I was excited, but not confident as Bamber Bridge had done a pretty good job on us this season. We had only beaten them in the cup and they had fielded a weakened side; in the three league games, we had to make do with two draws and a defeat. We seem to always play to their strengths, lumping the ball forward which is meat and drink to their four six foot plus defenders. Mind you I suppose that meant we owed them one and no better time than in a one off play off game.
The match started with the crowd in superb voice and Brig as the better side. We got away with it early on with a deflected shot beating Sam but thankfully clipping the top of the bar and going over.

As the half wore on, we started to slowly get a foot into the match, and took the lead thanks to the first bit of football we actually played in the game. The move started with Nuge knocking the ball across his own box to Fossie who passed the ball into Rory in the middle of the pitch. He passed the ball first time out to the wing where Adam Carden was waiting. He took the ball forwards, ran into the box and slammed the ball into the roof of the net. It wasn't the only roof that nearly came off, as Gigg gooned like it hadn't gooned since the infamous Quorn game. The goal did calm FC down a little. Brig was looking slightly the better team but another piece of superb football by FC doubled the lead. The ball was played out to Adam Carden who was playing like a demon on the wing, he cut into the box, drew the keeper and crossed to Rory who was stood in the middle all on his own and rolled the ball into the net.
At this point, special praise has to be given to Adam Carden who was playing superbly. His pace was giving nightmares to the Brig left back and he was finding space nearly every time he received the ball. In fact another one of his crosses found Ruddy in the box who shot over just before half time.
The interval arrived with a good two goal cushion for FC, but you had a feeling that Bamber Bridge weren't out of the game, and with only six minutes of the half gone, they had pulled a goal back when a freekick that in all honesty should have gone the way of FC was floated into the box and somehow Neil Zarac looped a header up and into the net. This sent the nerves round the crowd, and it could easily have been level when Brig went clean through, but Sam was equal to it and pulled off a save.
The game was certainly entertaining; it was everything you would want from a semi-final. Two committed teams going at it, decent attacking football and a referee who seemed incapable of giving the correct decisions. As we have seen time and again at Gigg, the ref seemed to be out to prove that the partisan crowd wasn't affecting him, by giving the away team every 50/50 decision.
This didn't seem to matter as Wright looked to have made the game safe with a deflected shot into the roof of the net on 69

minutes. Again the roof came off Gigg Lane as it seemed we were on our way to the play off final but as usual in typical United fashion, we were made to hang on as a cross was weakly punched out by Sam and Zarac volleyed his second goal of the game.
This ensured a nervy last eleven minutes with Brig going close with a shot into the side netting and Rory clattering their crossbar.
With the last few minutes seeming to last a lifetime the relief at the final whistle was palpable. The roar could probably be heard in the city centre as the players celebrated getting through to the final against Skelmersdale at Gigg Lane.
There was just time for the player to pick up the cup and their medals for finishing second. A cup and medals for finishing second!! Only in the Northern Premier League do you pick up medals and a trophy for finishing as runners up, how very strange.
So onto the last game, one last game, a game that would see FC promoted or having to settle for another season in NPL Div 1.

3rd May 2008
Unibond First Division North Play off final
FC United 4(Platt pen 41, Chadwick 51, Patterson 63 pen, C Baguley 80) Skelmersdale United 1
Attendance: 3258

I still don't like play offs. In fact I hate them even more now as they made me the most nervous I have ever been before a game. I have never in all the years of watching football felt as I did before this game. Even Barcelona 1999 pales into the shadows compared to this one. I mean there was plenty time between the semi-final and final to get yourself sorted for that game, there was also a league and FA cup win. Also flying out the day after the cup final and making the best part of a week of it helped as well, the thought being at least if we lose, we have the double to look back on and a decent holiday in Barca. With this game it

was all or nothing, all the hard work to get into this position possibly up in smoke thanks to just one game.
I don't think I was alone in having these nerves. Pre-match in the Swan watching the MUFC v West Ham game you could also sense the nerves. The pub was pretty full of people watching the game but the usual buzz and atmosphere was missing. The pub erupted as you would expect for each Utd goal but then it was back to the nervous watching of the game and the waiting till 3pm.
On walking down to the ground it was clear to see that the huge promotional push by some of the fans for this game had paid off as there were plenty of people milling about around the ground and queues of people at the turnstiles. A big well done to all who stood about after the Brig game or spent time in town handing out leaflets, your work paid off and you should be proud of yourselves.
The nerves, it seemed, had also got to the players as Skem started the better team. Cheered on by a decent away following of I would say a couple of hundred they took the game to FC and it was no surprise when they took the lead with a 25 yard free kick that flew past Sam into the net.
Not the start to calm the nerves.
As the half went on we got back into the game, Nuge heading against the bar and Rory having a shot blocked. It was frustrating to watch as you felt that if the players could get the ball down and play football the game was there to be won. The problem was too many of them looked as if they couldn't wait to get rid of the ball as soon as they received it.
Just before half time, and from nowhere we were quite literally handed a lifeline when the Skem captain pulled off a wonderful save on the line to prevent a certain FC goal. Sadly for Skem their captain was playing centre half and so the ref had no option but to award the penalty and send the player off, despite him claiming that he had headed the ball over. There followed a mêlée in which Adam Carden received a forehead on the nose for his trouble but thankfully this calmed down to allow Nicky Platt to place the ball on the spot.

Gigg went silent as everyone prayed that Platt could keep his calm and score the penalty. He could, he did and Gigg Lane erupted. Hopefully the nerves would be settled and the players could come out in the second half and express themselves in the way we know they can do.

These hopes were soon dashed as the players started as nervously in the second as they had done in the first. The defence made a couple of errors that thankfully didn't get punished as Skem started the half the better team. But as so often our skipper had other ideas and he met a free kick from the right with his head to put FC a goal up. Since he has come back from his injury for the second half of the season, Chaddy has been immense. It has showed how much his organising was missed before Christmas and how much his presence in the team really does settle the other players and give them the confidence to play.

Thankfully this goal seemed to knock a little bit of the stuffing out of Skem and we started to play some football and look the better team, and for once at Gigg, we got a little bit of luck with the referee and his decisions.

We were awarded a second penalty when a Skem defender fell onto the ball and was deemed to have handled it. It may have seemed a little harsh but it can't be denied that it was about time we actually got a big decision at Gigg Lane. As I have said before quite a few of the refs seem to come to Gigg and play the occasion not the game. They also seem as if they want to show they aren't swayed by the big crowd and in my view tend to go too far the opposite way and favour the away teams.

Anyway Nick Platt put the ball down and we all expected him to do the usual and place the ball low into the net. He didn't. For some reason he decided to go high and with power and blast the ball. Sadly he blasted the ball against the bar. As it was coming down, the referee spotted a push off the ball on Simon Carden and he awarded a third penalty to FC. This time Platt stood aside for Rory to take it. His penalty squirmed under the keeper and slowly rolled over the line to put FC 3-1 up.

Skem lost their shape and discipline after this and following a late challenge on Adam Carden, they were down to nine men as sub Leadbetter, who had only been on for about five minutes, was sent off for foul and abusive language towards the ref.
There was still time for a fourth FC goal thanks to a long range shot from Chris Baguley and an act of petulance from Rory who had been brought off for the scorer. He slumped off the pitch slowly with hunched shoulders, walked straight past Margy and threw his shirt to the ground before sitting on the bench. I can totally understand his frustration at being substituted, especially in such a big game, but it is a squad game and the manager has to make a decision who to bring off. We saw the same thing a few weeks ago with Stuart Rudd who did a similar thing. As I say it's understandable but slightly regrettable. Hopefully things were resolved after the game and Rory will be around to score his 100th FC goal, the fact that he was chasing that milestone may also have played a part in the incident.
The game then pretty much petered out with plenty of chances being missed by FC especially the Baguley brothers who seemed to be having their own little competition of who could miss the most chances. By my counting, Jamie won.
At the final whistle, the relief around Gigg, both on the pitch and in the stands was massive. The players celebrated a job well done and promotion to the NPL Premier Division and the promise of some fantastic trips ahead with the traditional spraying of champagne and the presentation of a glass vase to mark the play off victory.
After the game the recently reopened Pack Horse seemed to be the best place to get together and celebrate. It was a cracking night in the pub, a few of the players having a drink with the fans and even Steve Torpey showing his face and chatting to fans about life away from FC.
The night ended with many fans, including one or two who should know better, dancing on the tables in the pub to the likes of The Stone Roses, Happy Mondays and S Club 7.
All in all a fantastic ending to a superb season. One that was the typical clichéd rollercoaster ride with ups and downs both on

and off the pitch that will live on in the memory for a long long time.
They said it wouldn't last but the third season in the history of FC United of Manchester proved that not only could we cope with difficult times and adversity on and off the pitch, we positively thrived on it.

Epilogue

The season has been over for a month now, and as I sit in a bar in Marburg ahead of the post-season friendly game, it seems as good a time as any to look back and reflect on the season.
This season has made the club stronger there is no question about that. With the tougher time on the pitch and the many challenges off it, the club has an even more solid foundation than ever before. The first two seasons had been total successes. Getting a club off the ground, winning two titles and a cup, large crowds both at home and away, it couldn't have gone much better. The third season, in the Northern Premier League, would be the acid test. A higher level of football, more cup competitions to enter, uncertainty about how the crowds would hold up. It is safe to say that the team and management answered the playing side in no uncertain terms. A second place finish and promotion through the play off along with another cup win shows the progression that we have made, the games were tougher this season, more physical and at one point the season could have gone totally down the pan, but the determination and resilience of both the players and management team saw that the club had its third promotion in its short three season existence.
The crowds haven't been as high this season as the previous two, but if we are being honest that is to be expected. There was always a large novelty value attached to the NWCL seasons, FC was still new and raw, and of course the relatively easy nature of the majority of games made the fans come through the turnstiles. Promotion to the Unibond meant more games, and games further afield which in turn meant a stretch on the pocket. The games were also tenser affairs, so the amount of goals and at times, entertainment was less, meaning that maybe some fans from the first couple of seasons lost a little interest. Hopefully they attended the playoff games and found that some of the excitement was back. The weather also played its part with many games getting called off, resulting in the stupid and ridiculous fixture pile up at the start of April. Some of the away

games in that period over in Yorkshire saw the lowest crowds seen at competitive FC games, but the fact that there were even 400-500 at these games is testament to the loyalty shown to the club by its supporters.

If matters on the pitch took the difficulty levels up a notch, events off the pitch took them off the scale. We always knew that there would be difficult decisions to be made at some point with regards to games being moved for television coverage, I don't think we expected them to have to be made so soon and for a game screened on the internet. It was heart-warming and to the fans' and clubs credit that the boycott of the Curzon game was such a success. It showed that there is a line in the sand and as a club and a fanbase we are prepared not to cross that line, no matter how much we are pushed and derided for our decision.

The farce that was Burygate was all the more perplexing. Taking into account the date the game was due to be played and what that meant to the fans, the situation should never have occurred. The reasons that it did were of course covered earlier, but it is safe to say that in contrast to the Curzon boycott there were faults on both sides and in the end neither came out with much in the way of credit. Both these incidents have strengthened the club and brought together many of the fans in support of the club and hopefully there have been many lessons learned in order to avoid similar situations in the future.

There is no doubt that this season the club has achieved far more than could have been expected and has evolved more and more over the season and for that we should all be very proud.

No one ever said it was going to be easy, but it is safe to say that FC United of Manchester certainly didn't come unstuck in the Northern Premier League Div 1.

Trips on Glue Subscribers list

Beresford
Selvidge
Lamberts
Jump

Nugent

Bibby
Hamlett
Pagnam
l Hurst
an Hunt
bie Tunley
in Hunt
e Nolan
ron Cowell
yton Kennedy
on Howles
ard Langan
an Langan
in Randall
en Chadwick
ph Hunt
ny Thompson
tin K Andersen
ra
Prince
Tully
nonic Hunt
Barrow-FCUM
ON
progshop (ebay)

ny Selvidge
nor Brookes
id Winstanley

35. Katie Winstanley
36. Luis Delgardo
37. John Yates
38. James Boyd
39. Nick Hollowell
40. Jean Hollowell
41. Bill Hollowell
42. Matthew Charnock
43. Pete Smith
44. Tony Duree
45. Frank McElherron
46. Paul Cambridge
47. Mark van Spall
48. BigJimHolton
49. Paul Bamford
50. Peter Moulds
51. George Hurst
52. Daniel Wilson
53. Joshua Wilson
54. Irish Des
55. Andy Hughes
56. Alison Watt
57. Tony Barrow
58. Michael Holdsworth
59. Brian Hancock
60. Pauline England
61. Tony Vigus
62. John Roberts
63. BigJimHolton
64. Neil Boothman
65. Tim Williams
66. George Hayden
67. Paul Edwards
68. Paul Hayton
69. Darren O'Neill
70. Buckomcr
71. John Gallimore
72. Karl Ladley
73. Tim Browning
74. Karen Davies
75. Mark Bibby
76. Pete Luby
77. Dave Simpson
78. Kate Fox
79. Chris Boulderstone
80. Gary Newman
81. Jane Newman
82. Stuart Ward
83. Michael Richardson
84. John aka Spotsred
85. Karolina Doran
86. Robert Brady
87. Tanya Boothman
88. Gav Prince
89. Pete Cranmer
90. BigJimHolton
91. Gary Dyer
92. Ben Barrow
93. Jenga
94. Edwyn Noon
95. Louis Noon
96. Steve Doran
97. Alex Croft
98. Lucy Croft
99. Chris Johnson
100. Scott Fletcher
101. Jake Keys
102. Ross Keys
103. Bethany Keys
104. Scott Hayden
105. John England
106. Neil Thompson
107. Phil Bradbury
108. Anne and Claire Robinson
109. Pete Crowther
110. Gary Macey

the day fc united get in the football league

there'll be booze, crews, shouts an banter...songs serenade's,
mayhem an mantra...stumblers, fumblers, mumblers an
rumblers...one man bands an one night stands...there'll be weed,
speed an a double pie feed...an dancin an romancin...punks an
fallin down drunks...an roars, an whores an back street
scores...an people an places, kids with freckly faces an acne
traces
there'll be anoraks, with backpacks, an filo-fax a checkin their
facts...women singin, tits swingin an rafters ringin...an pubs an
clubs an chips in tubs, an kisses an hugs, an sharin of drugs
without any tugs...there'll be fakers, takers, movers an
makers...hawkers an street walkers...clerks, larks an fallin asleap
in parks
there'll be jibbers, fibbers, loners, losers, part time boozers,
sometime users...an honey's an bunnies a spendin yer
monies...there'll be scams an scrapes, jolly japes an narrow
escapes...there'll be "collyhurst road", an tales to be told by the
young an the old...there'll be moston an the heath, an broken
teeth an fans with belief...an plattin's an monsall's exercisin their
tonsils...there'll be a conga gettin longa an longa as the beat gets
stronga
it'll be sweet in manchester town that day

Mike Duff